CURE OR DISEASE? PRIVATE HEALTH INSURANCE IN CANADA

Steven Globerman
Aidan Vining
Simon Fraser University

Canadian Cataloguing in Publication Data

Globerman, Steven
      Cure or disease? private health insurance in Canada

(University of Toronto monograph series on public policy and public administration; no. 4)
ISBN 0-7727-8604-6

1. National health insurance — Canada. 2. Insurance, Health — Canada . 3. Medical care — Canada — Finance. 4. Health care reform — Canada. I. Vining, Aidan R. II. University of Toronto. Centre for Public Management. III Title. IV. Series.

HD7102.C2G56 1996   362.1'042'0971   C96-931515-5

Printed and bound in Canada.

TABLE OF CONTENTS

FOREWORD

The University of Toronto Centre for Public Management, enabled by a generous grant from the Donner Canadian Foundation, is in the midst of publishing a series of eight monographs on public-policy topics. Steven Globerman and Aidan Vining's *Cure or Disease? Private Health Insurance in Canada*, is the fourth to be published. Previous volumes include Barry Cooper's *The Klein Achievement*, Douglas Auld's *Expanding Horizons: Privatizing Post-Secondary Education*, and William J. Milne's *The McKenna Miracle: Myth or Reality?*

The University of Toronto Monograph Series' central theme is the diminishing role of government in Canada, particularly at the federal and provincial levels. In recent years, public criticism of government has become so widespread that it now reveals several distinct camps. For example, some of government's contemporary critics argue that when it comes to most major social and economic problems, government has proved, over the last quarter-century, that in its present form it is not the solution. The state, these critics argue, is an unsustainably costly or inherently inefficient means of providing certain welfare, education, health and other services. Much of what government now does is better left to private agencies, whether these agencies are for-profit or not-for-profit, and whether or not government retains a presence as purchaser, regulator, or voucher-provider.

Other critics of the state go further, urging that government is not only not the solution, it is actually the problem. Here the claim is that government programs are so prone to unintended consequences, perverse incentives and slippery-slope excesses, that they have actually *created* many of our social and economic ills. If we cut back the state's role in welfare-provision, these critics argue, many now dependent on welfare will rediscover their own market virtues of thrift and self-reliance. If we reduce the state's role in health-care, consumers will necessarily educate themselves on issues of prevention, self-diagnosis, and personal care and so reassume responsibilities they once carried for themselves before the state stepped in. If we diminish government's role in education, then parents and students, motivated to seek value for money, will force accountability and responsiveness on schools and universities.

Between these two positions — the negative one that government is not the solution, the positive one that government is actually the problem — there is much to argue about. More broadly, the move to roll back the state for whatever reason, though ascendant politically, is far from uncontroversial in Canadian public debate. One need not agree that the state ought to retrench, however, to accept that the state is retrenching — in Canada as in other welfare democracies. In the main, the authors in this series believe, as do most Canadians, that government in fact ought to retrench, particularly in the specific areas each discusses. But it is our intent that those who disagree with this proposition, either in general or in specific circumstances, will be stimulated by these monographs to respond, and so continue the debate.

The diminishing role of the state has, of course, been the theme of a number of other recent, and quite distinguished, monograph sets. There are, however, a couple of features which together may differentiate this endeavour from some other recent efforts.

First, each monograph, while not necessarily sole-authored, will take the form of a single essay, not a collection of papers. This format, longer than an article but much shorter than a book, allows authors to make an argument both sustained and succinct. Without this kind of an outlet, whether provided here or elsewhere, many important statements would be lost to public debate.

Second, the series itself has a comprehensive theme: the rollback of the state. Within this rubric some monographs address the issue of scaling back government as it pertains to broad policy areas such as health, education, regulation, and intergenerational equity in fiscal and social policy. *Cure or Disease? Private Health Insurance in Canada* falls into this class, as does Douglas Auld's recently-published *Expanding Horizons: Privatizing Post-Secondary Education*. Other monographs look at particular approaches different provinces have taken to contracting their public sectors. William J. Milne's *The McKenna Miracle* falls into this category as does Barry Cooper's *Klein Achievement*; we plan future volumes on Ontario and Fiscal Federalism and a comparative analysis that looks across provinces.

The Series, then, does not restrict itself to a particular policy field. Nor, therefore, do individual monographs address particular sub-issues within a confined topic area. Rather, the editors wanted free rein to select work that seemed the most pertinent to public debate over government retrenchment regardless of the specific topic. And we wanted to accord authors leeway to address their subjects in the broadest possible fashion.

Each monograph, written by academics but specifically for a broader audience that includes policy-makers, journalists, interest groups and citizens, is "peer reviewed". The arguments and recommendations made in each, however, are the sole responsibility of the author(s), and do not necessarily reflect the views of the University of Toronto Centre for Public Management. More information about the series can be obtained by contacting the Centre for Public Management at the Faculty of Management, University of Toronto, 105 St. George Street, Toronto, Ontario, M5S 3E6.

Andrew Stark
Editor
University of Toronto
Centre for Public Management

PREFACE

"Canada's health-care system is in crisis". For years this statement has been as much of a cliché among Canada's health-care suppliers as it has been taboo among Canada's health-care payers, our governments. What has changed in recent years is the awareness of Canada's health-care consumers who — in experiencing growing declines in the quality and quantity of services available to them — are beginning to demand, even initiate, a national debate on the future of Canada's health-care system.

"We take as a given", Steven Globerman and Aidan Vining write, "that most Canadians support and value the 'traditional' Medicare system... Our argument is simple: the risks of not allowing domestic private financing" into that system "outweigh the risks of allowing it".

Globerman and Vining argue that Canadians should be able to purchase private insurance coverage not just for peripheral medical services, as they currently can, but for the range of core medical services currently provided exclusively by the public system. And herein lies the novelty of their argument. Both traditional opponents and traditional advocates of a "two-tier" system argue that its introduction will ultimately destroy the public health-care system; they differ only as to whether this would be a good thing. Globerman and Vining argue that — within limits we are in no present danger of reaching — allowing Canadians to purchase medical services privately will not threaten, but will in fact bolster, a properly constituted public system.

After offering an overview of Canada's health-care system in the Introduction and Chapter One, Globerman and Vining proceed — in Chapter Two — to set out two basic steps toward reforming Canada's health-care system. First, because of fiscal pressures, the public system will have to cast off an array of services it currently underwrites, requiring consumers to pay for them out-of-pocket or cover them through private insurance. Upon exploring a range of alternatives, and recognizing that any such criteria will be prey to politicization and fraught with difficulties in economic and medical measurement, Globerman and Vining offer an approach for determining which services these should be.

Second, Globerman and Vining argue that when it comes to those services the public system should continue to underwrite — for example, core services such as cancer or heart surgery — Canadians ought to be able to purchase them privately as well. In Chapters Five and Six, Globerman and Vining address three basic concerns that such "two-tier" proposals always provoke. According to the first concern, as better-off Canadians find themselves able to purchase more and more of their health-care privately, their incentive to financially support the public system will erode. On the contrary, Globerman and Vining suggest, better-off Canadians are less likely to support the public system over time if, while it continues to decline in quality, they are precluded from supplementing this support with private care. Very wealthy Canadians, of course, will always be able to privately purchase needed health care in the United States anyway. A potentially much larger group of middle-income Canadians, however, may also find the public system increasingly inadequate to their needs but — unable to purchase such private care abroad — will begin to resent governmental attempts to prohibit them from accessing privately-financed care at home. More than anything, so Globerman and Vining argue, it is this phenomenon that could precipitate a serious drop in support for the public system. If middle-income Canadians "come to view the very existence of Medicare as a barrier to their attaining a minimally acceptable level of health", they will "have a strong incentive to lobby for its dismantling". Certainly in other countries those able to purchase some modicum of private insurance have continued to support their public systems. There "is no evidence", Globerman and Vining write, "that the existence of private insurance alternatives leads to the suppression or extinction of publicly financed alternatives".

The second concern surrounding private insurance has to do with subsidization; that is, with the possibility that physicians will use resources acquired under the public-insurance plan to provide services for which they will receive compensation under a patient's private plan. As Globerman and Vining note, this is "one of the major objections raised by critics of private clinics operating in Alberta, who argue that not all of the incremental costs of treating patients in the private clinics are incorporated in the extra-billings charged by the physicians". This problem, however, can be addressed through a system of implicit pricing — of a sort used by various public utilities — which would ensure that the incremental cost of the privately-provided service is not publicly subsidized.

As a side-benefit, Globerman and Vining argue, such a scheme would help deter physicians from giving preferential treatment to their privately-insured patients, another worry often expressed by those opposed to a two-tiered system. More generally, the concern that their access to private insurance will allow wealthier Canadians to bid away more qualified physicians, Globerman and Vining argue, assumes that the supply of "high quality" health-care providers is inelastic; that is, quite limited. This is a presumption they question. In any case, empirical evidence "supports the position that physicians do not abandon the publicly financed program for private schemes under mixed financing regimes".

Finally, while the introduction of private insurers could lead to administrative inefficiencies — as many insurers will have to duplicate for themselves the procedures the government alone now provides — Globerman and Vining argue that it could also lead to administrative efficiencies within both the public and private systems as a result of increased competition.

There is, Globerman and Vining conclude in Chapter Seven, ample room for the growth of private financing within the current Canadian public system. As they put it, the risks of not introducing such elements outweigh the risks of introducing them. Certainly, they caution, a "*significant* reduction in public-sector funding of health care would lead to reduced access on the part of lower-income groups" to medically necessary services, "a result deemed by most, if not all Canadians, to be undesirable". But, they point out, "any such reduction would be the outcome of a policy decision to reduce government expenditures and not the necessary result of wealthier Canadians buying some of their health care through private markets for insurance".

In sum, Globerman and Vining offer a valuable contribution to the emerging public debate over Canada's health-care system. They join discussion in a timely way by arguing that a more cost-effective public system, and a more permissive public policy stance toward private financing, would lead to the kind of health-care regime most in conformity with the values Canadians cherish.

ACKNOWLEDGEMENTS

The authors would like to thank Betty Chung for word processing assistance. They also thank two anonymous reviewers for many helpful comments.

INTRODUCTION

Concerns about reduced access to medical care are front-page news in Canada (Cernetig, 1995:A1). In particular, there is a growing belief that financial pressures are inevitably leading to reductions in the funding of Canada's Medicare system at the federal and provincial government levels. Reduced funding, in turn, is seen as leading to a reduction in the supply of services covered by Medicare. The outcome of any such reductions in funding is a hotly debated topic. One point of view, represented by recent pronouncements of the federal government, is that reductions in funding can be offset by efficiency gains including the elimination of "unnecessary" treatments and procedures. As such, reductions in funding will not necessitate making any additional "hard choices": universal coverage will continue as before for all medical treatments and procedures that are necessary. An alternative point of view holds that funding reductions inevitably entail reductions in access to treatments that have some medical value. In this view, it will be necessary to make hard choices. Contentious as the word is, this means rationing in some shape or form. It may, therefore, be preferable to have an explicit model of rationing that is arrived at through some process of public dialogue, rather than simply "muddling through". Reform Party Leader Preston Manning, for example, has called for the division of current medical practices into "core" and "non-core" services. Core services would be guaranteed and financed by federal and provincial governments. Non-core services would be financed through "more flexible" combinations of private insurance and user-pay schemes (Delacourt, 1995:A4).

As a practical matter, access to medical care in Canada is already rationed in the sense that Medicare does not cover all medical services currently offered by the health-care professions. Currently, the major form of rationing in Canada is queuing (Ramsay and Walker, 1995). Indeed, if by rationing we mean that at least some individuals cannot or do not obtain all of the medical care they would like to receive, then rationing has always been a fact of life under all types of health-care delivery systems. As Richard Lamm, former governor of Colorado, puts it: "The search for a health-care system that does not ration, like the search for the judge that does not err, is not only futile, but also demeaning to a thoughtful people" (Lamm, 1992:1513).

A basic premise of this study is that Canadians currently enjoy less than universal access to medical services under Medicare, either because some services are not covered at all, or because many services covered are not available "on demand" by medical practitioners acting as agents for their patients. While it may be contentious to label such deviations from universal access as rationing, such usage is consistent with the spirit of the relevant literature and the thrust of the policy debate surrounding health-care funding. Rationing reflects any situation in which demand is greater than supply and (therefore) some mechanism must be invoked to allocate the available supply. To the extent that waiting lists for procedures and treatments allocate scarce capacity (at any point in time) among competing uses, they serve as a rationing device. To the extent that services and products such as pharmaceuticals, wheelchairs, eyeglasses, acupuncture and so forth are not covered under Medicare, prices and the willingness-to-pay of consumers serve as the rationing device.

Another premise of this study is that pressures will increase to further reduce the range (and possibly the quality) of products and services covered under the Medicare Plan and/or to accept even longer queues for specific procedures. No predictions are offered about whether funding reductions will be absolute or relative to gross domestic product (GDP) growth, nor about the magnitude of any funding reduction. However, pressures on health-care administrators to maintain or increase output at lower than historical rates of funding are likely to grow inexorably (Marzouk, 1991). One important consequence will be a growing demand for more "private-sector" alternatives to Medicare. The broad policy issues raised are therefore: (1) to the extent that the demand for publicly-funded medical services is (or will be) greater than the supply of those services, what is the appropriate policy (or policies) to allocate scarce capacity among competing uses, especially in the public sector?; (2) should greater reliance be placed upon the private sector to provide services? This study addresses these two broad issues.

The study proceeds as follows. Chapter One provides additional perspective on the main policy issues addressed in this study, including an overview of the financing pressures facing Canada's Medicare system and the prospects for efficiency gains to mitigate these emerging pressures. Chapter Two identifies a range of alternative policies to allocate increasingly scarce (relative to demand) health-care resources among competing uses, that is, rationing. Chapter Three discusses the social welfare criteria that might be employed in evaluating these alternatives. Chapter Four assesses the viability of using cost-effectiveness criteria to allocate health resources. Chapters Five and Six consider the issue of whether and how increased private financing of health care would affect the Medicare system and assess the social welfare implications of a larger role for private financing of health care in Canada: Chapter Five considers the theoretical issues, while Chapter Six reviews the empirical evidence from a number of countries. Chapter Seven provides conclusions and policy recommendations.

CHAPTER ONE

An Overview Of Canada's Medicare System

It is common in the press to label the Canadian health-care system as being in financial "crisis", with the implication that there will be significant reductions in the extent of coverage of the publicly-funded system. However, as Stoddart *et. al.* (1993) point out, there has been conflict over health-care funding in Canada ever since Medicare was introduced over 20 year ago. Indeed, the Canadian system is *designed* to produce tension between health-care providers and the provincial governments acting on behalf of taxpayers. Specifically, governments can be expected to try to reduce funding levels — or growth rates of funding — while health-care providers can be expected to argue that any such efforts will result in significant reductions in the supply of necessary health-care services with adverse consequences for the health status of the population.

A Profile of Finances and Expenditures for Canadian Health Care

Public concern about a crisis in Canada's health care sector have arguably been heightened by Prime Minister Chretien's statements that spending on health care as a share of GDP in Canada is higher than in other developed countries, except the United States, and that it is an appropriate public policy goal to reduce Canada's ratio so that it is more in line with less expensive European models (Coutts, 1995:A5) (See Table 1.1). In addition, it has been noted that the growth rate of Canadian expenditures of 17 percent during the 1980s in inflation-adjusted dollars has been high, lagging behind growth rates only in the United States and Ireland (OECD, 1993).

Budgetary pressure on the provinces has also been heightened by the federal government's February 1995 budget which cut deeply into transfer payments to the provinces (Greenspon, 1995:A1). Until 1993, the federal government accounted for almost 25 percent of health care funding, of which around 22 percent took the form of transfers to the provinces. Provincial funds accounted for around 46 percent of all health care funding (Health and Welfare Canada, 1993). Given the precarious state of provincial government budgets, provincial governments may have little choice but to pass on these cuts as cuts to spending on social services, including health care. Suggestions by Premier Klein that Alberta may

Table 1.1

Share of Total Health Expenditure in Total Domestic Expenditure, 1991	
Country	**Share**
United States	13.3
Canada	9.9
France	9.1
Germany	9.1
Finland	8.9
Sweden	8.8
Netherlands	8.7
Australia	8.6
Austria	8.5
Norway	8.4
Iceland	8.3
Italy	8.3
Belgium	8.1
Switzerland	8.0
Ireland	8.0
New Zealand	7.7
Denmark	7.0
Japan	6.8
Luxembourg	6.6
United Kingdom	6.6
Spain	6.5
Portugal	6.2

Source: Organization for Economic Cooperation and Development (1993:18).

need to deinsure some procedures covered by Medicare, while providing others on a user-pay basis, are seen by some as the proverbial "thin edge of the wedge".[1]

To be sure, there is nothing inevitable about reductions of health-care expenditures by the provinces. They could spend more on health care and less on other activities such as education. Whether politicians have the inclination to make deep cuts in other publicly-funded programs in favour of health-care programs is an open question. For most provinces, health care is already their major expenditure category. In several provinces, it is almost half of total government expenditures (Health and Welfare Canada, 1993). The aging of Canada's population also has conflicting implications for public financing decisions. On the one hand, elderly Canadians constitute a growing group with an interest in maintaining, or increasing, health-care spending. On the other hand, as older Canadians use a disproportionate share of health-care resources, the aging of the Canadian population suggests that provincial governments must inevitably consider changes to health-care financing if provincial deficits and indebtedness levels are to be reduced.

It is not just that aggregate health budgets are likely to be held constant or decline while demand remains constant. Demand will continue to increase. Costs are also likely to increase. Demand can be expected to increase for two primary reasons. First, there is the increasing number of seniors. Older patients require more costly health care. The elderly use health-care resources much more intensively than other Canadians. The 65 to 74 age group uses approximately 2.5 times the number of services per capita as the 15 to 44 age group. These utilization rates are even higher for hospital and long-term facilities, which are typically the most expensive component of health care (Crichton, Hsu, and Tsang, 1994:141). Second, medical innovation can be expected to continue for the foreseeable future. This creates new products which, quite rationally, consumers want. Ironically, some of this innovation exacerbates the first problem. As Gordon Tullock (1995:78) points out "... there are so many more older people now because of the superior treatment of the lesser diseases of the younger part of life...". At least the projected increase in demand is fairly easily understood, and is, therefore, at least acknowledged. A projected increase in costs is less well understood, even though it is probably part of a process that has been going on for approximately two hundred years. It stems from the fact that health care is a relatively labour-intensive service activity and, therefore, relatively stagnant in terms of productivity growth over time (Baumol, 1967). "Stagnant services have an inherent tendency to rise in price at a (compounded) rate faster than the economy's overall rate of inflation... [and] ...to use a share of the economy's labor inputs that grows at a rate disproportionately larger than the growth in the share of the economy's output" (Baumol, Blackman, and Wolff, 1989:124).

To reiterate, it is not the purpose of this analysis to make detailed predictions about future levels of public funding on health care. Nor is its purpose to speculate about how new technologies may affect demand for health care or whether efficiency improvements can offset financing pressures, although the issue of "necessary" versus "unnecessary" medical procedures is addressed in a later section. The main point is that pressures on the universality of Medicare are more likely to increase than to decrease in the foreseeable future. As a consequence, decisions about what procedures and treatments will be covered under Medicare, and for which Canadians, will become increasingly incumbent upon policy makers. It

17

is, of course, true that such policy considerations are important even if there were projections for increasing health-care budgets, since they are relevant to the pursuit of efficiency and equity.

Current Limitations on Universality: Waiting and Non-Coverage

In outlining the current status of, and prospects for, Canada's health-care system, it is useful to briefly review the current limitations on Medicare. Such limitations take a variety of forms. One limitation takes the form of waiting for treatments and procedures. To the extent that queuing reduces productivity through physical infirmity, worry or other factors, it imposes a real, if implicit, cost on the economy. It also implies psychological costs for individuals. Differences in waiting exist not only across procedures, but also across geographical regions. Table 1.2 reports the median number of weeks patients waited to see specialists in 1994, by specialty and by province. Table 1.3 reports the total expected waiting time from a GP referral to time of treatment.[2] There is substantial debate surrounding the methodology used to obtain the estimates reported in Tables 1.2 and 1.3. There is also debate surrounding the appropriate interpretation of these estimates. For example, it is unclear how much waiting results from overall "excess demand" for specialty services and

Table 1.2

Median 1994 Patient Wait to See a Specialist After Referral from a G.P. (in weeks)												
Specialty	BC	AB	SK	MB	ON	PQ	NB	NF	NS	PE	NT	CAN
Plastic Surgery	5.5	9.0	7.5	10.0	4.0	4.0	5.0	12.0	6.5	4.0	—	5.7
Gynaecology	2.0	4.0	2.8	2.5	4.0	3.0	6.0	3.5	7.0	4.3	4.0	3.7
Ophthalmology	3.0	2.5	8.0	10.5	6.0	6.0	10.0	4.0	5.0	4.0	1.0	5.9
Otolaryngology	2.0	6.5	1.0	3.5	3.0	3.0	3.0	1.2	5.0	4.0	5.0	3.2
General Surgery	2.3	2.0	2.0	2.0	2.0	2.0	2.0	2.0	2.2	1.0	2.0	2.0
Neurosurgery	5.5	10.5	6.0	11.0	12.0	8.0	12.0	8.0	3.3	—	—	9.8
Orthopaedic Surgery	10.0	7.5	5.0	12.0	9.0	6.0	8.0	6.0	11.0	5.0	12.0	8.3
Cardiovascular Surgery	2.5	2.0	2.0	1.5	2.5	2.5	0.5	1.0	—	—	—	2.0
Urology	4.0	4.0	1.0	3.0	4.0	4.0	3.5	3.5	3.8	3.0	—	3.8
Internal Medicine	2.0	2.0	2.0	2.0	3.0	2.0	3.0	2.0	3.0	5.0	5.0	2.4
Radiation Oncology	2.5	1.3	1.0	2.0	2.0	1.0	1.0	1.0	1.0	—	—	1.9
Medical Oncology	2.0	1.3	1.0	1.8	1.8	1.5	0.5	—	1.5	0.5	—	1.7
Weighted Median	3.5	3.8	3.0	4.1	4.3	3.5	4.8	3.1	4.4	3.6	4.7	3.9

Source: Ramsay and Walker (1995:25).

Table 1.3

Total Expected Waiting Time from G.P. Referral to Treatment, 1994 (in weeks)										
Specialty	BC	AB	SK	MB	ON	PQ	NB	NF	NS	PE	CAN
Plastic Surgery	17.9	18.1	13.6	22.9	9.4	8.5	13.5	26.0	38.1	25.1	15.5
Gynaecology	9.0	11.3	10.1	9.4	8.7	8.5	15.7	6.6	14.0	22.9	10.2
Ophthalmology	12.6	9.8	25.9	21.8	18.9	15.2	19.4	7.3	17.8	9.1	17.2
Otolaryngology	12.9	12.5	8.9	14.0	8.9	6.9	18.1	5.7	16.7	24.5	11.0
General Surgery	8.2	5.6	6.8	5.5	5.1	5.2	5.4	6.2	5.7	10.3	5.8
Neurosurgery	10.8	15.3	12.4	27.3	17.1	16.1	25.7	13.6	7.8	—	16.4
Orthopaedic Surgery	25.7	20.2	20.2	24.5	19.6	15.0	27.5	13.7	37.4	54.4	21.3
Cardiovascular Surgery (elective)*	15.3	16.0	10.7	121.5	10.5	7.2	21.5	25.0	24.0	—	29.0
Urology	11.4	7.0	4.8	6.2	7.6	8.5	10.9	6.7	8.2	13.6	8.1
Internal Medicine	5.1	4.8	4.9	4.7	6.7	4.2	6.4	5.9	6.3	6.9	5.5
Radiation Oncology	8.5	3.8	2.0	8.0	5.0	7.0	4.0	3.0	5.0	—	6.3
Medical Oncology	3.0	1.8	1.5	2.0	2.6	2.3	1.0	—	1.8	1.5	2.5
Weighted Median	10.9	9.1	9.7	11.0	9.3	8.2	13.1	7.5	11.7	16.6	9.7

*Weighted median does not include pacemaker waits.
Source: Ramsay and Walker (1995:41).

how much from bottlenecks stemming from "imbalances" in patient caseloads across specialists.

An optimistic interpretation of the data in Tables 1.2 and 1.3 is that priorities are being implicitly set by policymakers through their resource allocation decisions, although the criteria underlying the priorities are unclear without detailed study. A more realistic interpretation is that access to health care varies both by geographical location as well as idiosyncratically by nature of treatment sought.[3] For example, it is not obvious that plastic surgery should have a higher priority than neurosurgery. Do shorter waiting times reflect higher funding priorities? These variations are useful to bear in mind when considering objections to allowing greater private financing of health care on grounds that it will make for inequities in access to health care. There are already marked inequities under the existing financing regime.

Limitations on universality also exist in the form of implicit charging for some health-related services, or, equivalently, a lack of coverage under the existing Medicare Plan. For example, in all provinces doctor visits are free, but the drugs prescribed at that visit may not be — depending upon the patient's age, income and province of residence. Hospital care is free, but not the ambulance that may have brought one there. Drugs used in hospital are free, but patients who use the same drugs after discharge from hospital must pay for them. A tooth extracted by an oral surgeon is not free under Medicare, unless it is done in a hospital. And so on. For further details, see Evans, Barer, Stoddart, and Bhatia (1994), and Deber, Mhatie, and Baker (1994).

A broad perspective on the coverage of health-care services in Canada is provided by Table 1.4. Clearly, the bulk of health-care expenditures in Canada is paid for under publicly-financed schemes, given the dominance of expenditures on hospital and physicians' services. There is some indication of deinsuring of hospital services, and this trend would be more noticeable with more recent data. Moreover, the effective rate of public financing can be expected to decline if pharmaceuticals continue to increasingly substitute for surgery. The main point underscored by Table 1.4 is that if the argument is that *any* amount of private financing sets Canada on a "slippery slope" towards a U.S.-style health financing regime, the slide has already begun. However, in a later section it will be argued that the "slippery slope" is an inappropriate, indeed misleading, metaphor.

Table 1.4

Major Categories of Health Care Spending by Sources of Financing				
	Public		**Private**	
	Millions	**%**	**Millions**	**%**
Hospital Services				
1987	17,037	89.0	2,116	11.0
1991	23,085	88.5	3,010	11.5
Physicians' Services				
1987	7,344	95.6	335	4.4
1991	9,736	96.0	405	4.0
Pharmaceuticals				
1987	1,424	24.1	4,497	75.9
1991	2,546	27.6	6,684	72.4
Capital				
1987	1,571	70.3	661	29.7
1991	1,626	67.9	787	32.1

Source: Tholl (1984:Table 6).

Implicit Versus Explicit Decision Making

While one can try to rationalize observed patterns of coverage and non-coverage of services under Medicare where waiting might be considered a manifestation of incomplete coverages, it seems clear that the observed patterns cannot be said to reflect the outcomes of explicit public policy decision-making. If the patterns are not completely *ad hoc*, neither are they the result of explicitly derived and articulated public policy rules to curtail Medicare access. If financing cutbacks do lead to increased waiting for Medicare services and/or reductions in specific services (or types of services), some specific pattern of costs and benefits will be imposed on the population. Alternative rationing schemes would undoubtedly impose different patterns of costs and benefits. As budgets tighten, policy-makers are being increasingly challenged to justify any specific pattern of costs and benefits. Such justification, in turn, will require that any rationing rule have broad public support. More generally, a number of observers have argued that the effectiveness of any rationing approach depends upon general public agreement about the approach(es) chosen (Blank, 1992).

As limitations on "effective" universal access grow, one can anticipate increased public concern about the "fairness" and the efficiency of current *de facto* rationing policies. For example, concerns about unfairness were expressed when then-Premier of Quebec, Robert Bourassa, went to the National Institute of Health in Maryland for immediate treatment of malignant skin cancer, rather than using the Canadian system with, presumably, the attendant waiting time. Academics have also raised concerns about the underlying fairness of the current pattern of exceptions to no user charges (see Stoddart *et. al.*, 1993). This suggests that the (to-date) largely academic and informal debate about how to allocate scarce health-care resources among competing uses will become both more public and more political.[4]

CHAPTER TWO

A Framework For Understanding Alternative Methods For Providing Health Care

The purpose of this section is to provide a framework for understanding the alternative methods of providing health care. A simple framework is developed which is linked, in a preliminary way, to actual methods of deciding which treatments will be made available; whether, for example, this is a function of individual physician discretion, private health insurers' willingness to cover a procedure, or governments' willingness to actually provide a certain treatment. Later the framework is broadly linked to a variety of philosophical, or normative, positions on the provision of health care, such as libertarianism, utilitarianism, or Rawlsianism.

Dimensions of the Framework: Source of Financing and Explicitness of Rationing

The framework focuses on two dimensions. The first is the source of financing of the system — this can be private, public, or mixed. The second is the degree of explicitness related to the criteria that are used to allocate health-care treatment. This can range from completely explicit to completely implicit. These two dimensions are analyzed in detail, because as Robert Blank (1992:1573) points out, these two factors largely determine the role and type of rationing that can occur: "Some forms of rationing imply or necessitate government involvement, either direct or indirect, while others fail to distinguish between private and public sector choices. This distinction is critical to a clarification of how current health-care options differ from past ones". These two dimensions are combined in Figure 2.1, to produce a number of potential allocation mechanisms (five or six, depending on one's viewpoint). We describe these in detail below after explaining the two dimensions, or "axes".

1. Source of Financing The financing source for health care can either be public, private or a mix of the two (Hurst, 1992: Besley and Gouveia, 1992). It is important to emphasize that (for the broad framework) the critical element in health-care rationing is likely to be the degree of public financing, rather than the degree of direct government "production" of services (Besley and Gouveia, 1994:201; Vining and Weimer, 1990). That is, the system of *financing* tends to drive what gets provided to whom.[1]

Figure 2.1
Financing Source

		Public	Mixed	Private
Rationing Mechanism	**Implicit**	**Single** **Multi** Physician Discretion Administrative Discretion Queueing	Less Conflict Between Public & Private Components	Mainly Price
	Explicit	Committee Rankings Cost-Effectiveness Ranking User Charges Co-Payments "Insurance" Premiums	Conflict Between Public & Private Components	"Spot" or Insurance Mandated Services (Mandated Cross-Subsidy)

To be sure, the efficiency with which health-care goods and services are produced does indirectly affect the extent to which rationing is necessary. This has, indeed, led many to focus on production "waste" as the core issue in health-care reform. But it is unlikely to be the whole story, or even the most important part of the story. This stems from the fact that the combination of public financing and private provision of health services faces many of the same efficiency problems as fully public systems (that is, systems which rely on public provision as well as public financing). Health-care provision (although not necessarily many of the ancillary services) involves many highly complex services and, therefore, information asymmetry between the government financier and the actual suppliers of health services. There may also, in many circumstances, be high asset specificity and low contestability in the health-care "market" (Globerman and Vining, 1996). High asset specificity means that once resources are committed to a specified health-care use, they cannot be easily redeployed to other uses. Low contestability implies that there are few other potential suppliers of services. The presence of either one, but especially the combination, suggests that both government provision or contracted-out provision will present similar problems — in particular, opportunistic behaviour on the part of suppliers that raises costs. For example, to counteract the risk of such opportunistic behaviour, the government may contract with more than one supplier even though this means none of the suppliers can produce at efficient scale.

It is important to emphasize that private financing does not necessarily, or usually, mean direct out-of-pocket payments by individuals. Most private financing in most countries is through some form of private insurance (Wagstaff and Doorslaer, 1992; Glaser, 1991).[2]

There are two main forms of public financing of health-care: social insurance schemes and tax-financed schemes. Most countries with social insurance systems based them on statutory sickness funds which are usually jointly governed by employees and employers. They are overseen and tightly regulated by governments. Risks are pooled in the fund and premiums are income-related over some range. Membership is compulsory for certain groups (for example, those with lower incomes) and in some cases cover virtually the entire population. Funds are organized along a variety of lines including by industry, geographical location or occupational status. Tax-financed schemes are based upon the state insuring health care and financing it as part of the budget. Under tax-financing, responsibility for production/provision can either be vested in government or delegated to largely private (mainly non-profit) suppliers, as in Canada (OECD, 1995:22).

Exclusive public financing is almost impossible to achieve or enforce because it is extremely difficult to prevent individuals who wish to purchase private health care on the margin from actually doing so, even in a system that putatively bans all forms of private health care.[3] Moreover, the uniformity generally characteristic of publicly-financed services ensures that a significant number of individuals have both incentives and resources to search and pay for services that augment the publicly-funded package. However, whether because of these practical reasons, or because of more fundamental normative reasons, almost no developed country has attempted to completely ban private supply. Presumably, the higher the perceived quality and quantity of services provided by public financing, the more limited the incentives to search for supplementary services outside the public system.

While a compulsory publicly-funded health-care strategy might not totally choke off demand for private care, it might effectively choke off domestic supply of private health-care alternatives, given that there are much greater indivisibilities in supply than in demand. For example, private insurers may need a critical mass of customers to offer insurance at "reasonable" prices, and this critical mass may not be available in the presence of highly subsidized publicly-funded insurance. Historically, Canada may have been one of the countries that was closest to a purely public system, although the United Kingdom was quite close before the evolution of a privately-financed hospital sector (Abel-Smith, 1981). Currently, Norway is probably the closest. That is, Norway has essentially no private financing of health care (see Table 2.1). However, even holding constant quality and quantity, the supply situation in any given jurisdiction can change, especially if non-domestic sources of supply become viable. For example, transportation costs and other transaction costs of going to other countries for health treatment, most obviously to the United States in the Canadian context, have gone down, implying that potential demand for insurance to fund treatment in other countries may increase. Of course, in practice quality can never be held completely constant if health care is at least somewhat like other goods that consumers purchase — quality is "in the eye of the beholder". Whether as a result of explicit policy or because of other factors, quite a few national governments have, in fact, lowered their share of health expenditures relative to the private sector during the 1980s (OECD, 1993).

Similarly, totally private financing is rare. Private insurance schemes are characterized primarily by setting premiums on the basis of their risk characteristics. Only two countries (the United States and Switzerland) have private insurers covering major health-care risks for the bulk of the population, although in Switzerland insurers are heavily regulated and required to provide community rather than individual risk-rating (OECD, 1995:22). The United States, which has the greatest degree of private financing among developed countries, devotes considerable government expenditures at the federal, state and local government levels to health care. OECD estimates indicate that the public sector share in total health expenditures in the U.S. rose from 24.5 percent in 1960 to 43.9 percent in 1991 (OECD, 1993). It should be noted that employer contributions to employee health care benefits are tax-deductible. Hence, the total publicly-funded share of health care in the United States, including the value of the relevant tax expenditures, is higher than the 43.9 percent share reported above. Some developing countries may be closest to complete private financing, especially if one includes charitable and aid financing in the private financing category (Mujinja, Urassa, and Mynika, 1993).

While totally "pure" private or public systems are rare, or perhaps even non-existent, elucidating the characteristics of the pure forms is useful because they clarify the components of the more complex mixed systems. Mixed systems are more complex than either public or private financed systems in two distinct ways. First, and most obviously, they are descriptively more complex because of the multiple financing sources. Second, and much more importantly for the purposes of this analysis, different forms of financing — especially those where a substitution is

Table 2.1

The Public Share in Total Expenditure on Health (Percent - 1991)	
Country	Percent
Australia	67.8
Austria	67.1
Belgium	88.9
Canada	72.2
Denmark	81.5
Finland	80.9
France	73.9
Germany	71.8
Iceland	87.0
Ireland	75.8
Italy	77.5
Japan	72.0
Luxembourg	91.4*
Netherlands	73.1
New Zealand	78.9
Norway	96.6
Portugal	61.7*
Spain	82.2
Sweden	78.0
Switzerland	68.3
UK	83.3
US	43.9

*1990 values
Source: OECD (1993:252).

occurring between public and private financing (in either direction) — affect each other. In other words, there are potential interactions between the two (Joseph and Flynn, 1988). These interactions can range from the highly macro-level to a quite micro-level (for examples, see Carrere, 1991; Naylor, 1988). The consequences of these interactions are complex and difficult to predict. For example, at the most macro-level, does the mere presence of privately-financed facilities or private health insurance reduce the level of political support for publicly-financed health care? At a more micro-level, does the presence of private sector participants in some places encourage the public system to "compete" more vigorously in these areas, and commit more resources, relative to elsewhere?[4]

2. **The Explicitness of Rationing** Rationing of health care can either

be explicit or implicit (Mechanic, 1992; Blank, 1992) where the terms reference the degree to which criteria are publicly known. If the rationing is sufficiently implicit, health-care consumers may even be unaware that rationing is taking place (Annas, 1995). Indeed, a health system may be designed in such a way, and providers may act in ways, that deliberately obscure the presence of rationing. An additional layer of complexity is added by the fact that a given health system may have different degrees of explicitness for the rationing of different kinds of procedures. For example, most countries have been forced to be relatively explicit about the allocation criteria for transplant organs as demand far exceeds supply (Blumstein and Sloan, 1989). Moreover, potential transplant recipients have the requisite incentives to demand explicitness (Schwindt and Vining, 1986).[5]

Combinations of Financing and Explicitness

Having outlined the two major dimensions, specific combinations of financing and explicitness can be examined. The four simplest combinations are: public financing-implicit rationing criteria, public financing-explicit rationing criteria, private financing-implicit rationing criteria and private financing-explicit rationing criteria. Then mixed systems are briefly considered. Of course, the fact that most systems are mixed adds an additional level of complexity. A health system, for example, may employ implicit rationing criteria in its publicly-financed component and explicit rationing criteria in its privately-financed component. Issues relating to mixed systems are examined in greater detail in subsequent sections.

1. **Public Financing-Implicit Rationing Criteria**   The first combination examined is public financing with implicit rationing. There are essentially three ways of implicitly rationing with public financing: (1) individual or small group physician discretion (either in terms of primary care and/or hospital treatment), (2) decentralized administrative and bureaucratic discretion, and (3) informal queuing; that is, where there is no explicit ranking of procedures and individuals. If there are explicit queue rankings it is more useful to regard queuing as an explicit rationing mechanism. The emphasis on "individual", "decentralized" and "informal" is critical since physicians or administrators can also be involved in explicit rationing, for example, by participating in centralized, formal allocation mechanisms.

There is a continuum of allocation rules that makes any simple dichotomization between explicit and implicit an oversimplification. It is certainly possible to fashion rationing rules that have the outward appearance of explicitness, but which do not, in fact, significantly reduce decentralized decision-makers' discretion.

As mentioned at the beginning of this section, rationing takes on meaning only if a government is unwilling to meet all demand. In practice, this requires some form of effective budget-capping. Thus, the rationing aspects of the mechanisms just described may not, at least initially, be very apparent if budget controls on health-care expenditures (that is, some form of capping) are "eased in".

The combination of public financing and caps, with resulting implicit allocation, has perhaps been the dominant strategy in European-Union countries. The imposition of cash-limited budgets, target budgets, or quotas over the whole health sector or important parts of it, have proved to be particularly effective capping procedures (Abel-Smith and Mossialos, 1994:90). This form of implicit rationing was, for example, the dominant mode under the British National Health Service until the 1990s, when the introduction of regional, fixed budgets and other reforms have pushed the system to more explicit rationing.[6] While on the surface public financing with implicit rationing criteria may seem unattractive, it has widespread support. There appear to be two groups of supporters: those who are prepared to openly defend implicit rationing (Mechanic, 1992) and those who end up *de facto* defending implicit rationing by their rejection of all of the other feasible combinations.[7] Arguably, the latter are in the majority in Canada.

The evidence is that reliance on implicit rationing is decreasing in Canada. This may simply reflect the fact that budget restrictions are "biting" and that while decisionmakers and patients were prepared to accept implicit rationing when the consequences were not too major, they are no longer prepared to do so. Certainly regionalization with fixed budgets appears to be encouraging a greater willingness to consider explicit rationing decisions. It may also reflect greater recognition of the emerging availability of evaluative tools and evidence for making allocation decisions.

2. **Public Financing-Explicit Rationing Criteria** Explicit rationing exists to some extent in the current Canadian system. One manifestation is the variations in provincial health coverage (Boothe and Johnstone, 1993:7). However, explicit criteria for allocating health-care resources has played a marginal role in Canada until the last few years. Public financing combined with explicit criteria is a combination that will be considered in detail later in this analysis. The primary reason for this focus is twofold. First, several other developed countries with primarily

publicly-funded systems are moving in the direction of adopting explicit allocation criteria. Second, Canadian policymakers are already being challenged to deal with explicit allocation criteria. This is most clear in provinces such as Saskatchewan and British Columbia which are moving to regionalization with global budgets that are essentially fixed.

Governments have a number of (possible) mechanisms to explicitly ration health-care access. The major mechanisms are: (1) committee guidelines, or rankings, of eligible procedures (with some combination of politicians, health-care providers, administrators and the general public making up the committees); (2) committee-derived cost-effectiveness rankings, with some explicit cut-off point; (3) user charges or co-payments for some or all services for those above some minimum income level and/or employment status (these may be described as "insurance" schemes, but are essentially taxes); and (4) voluntary, but subsidized, insurance premiums.

In using such mechanisms, there are essentially two criteria that can be used: efficiency, equity or some combination of the two. For example, one method of combining the two would be age cohort-based (an equity criterion) cost-effectiveness rankings (an efficiency criterion). While the primary normative "push" for explicit rationing mechanisms has been improved efficiency in the allocation of health-care resources, the actual mechanisms being chosen incorporate distributional factors, as will be described below. Those explicitly favouring a consideration of both efficiency and distributional (equity) concerns have tended naturally to gravitate to allocational committees with broad, relatively undefined, mandates which allow for "flexibility" in terms of applying criteria (Hadorn, 1988; Lamm, 1992). Such committees, therefore, can be thought of as being on the boundary between implicit and explicit rationing.

We exclude from consideration, for the purposes of this analysis, corrupt criteria, such as "who you know", although they may be relevant to the choice both between public and private financing and the choice between implicit and explicit rationing in some contexts. Implicit rationing, for example, is much more susceptible to corrupt allocation criteria, as the former communist-bloc shows.

When health care is privately-financed, the distinction between implicit and explicit rationing becomes less obvious, but it still has relevance.

3. **Private Financing-Implicit Rationing Criteria**   The rationing imposed by a market is generally explicit, that is, the willingness to pay market prices. However, there are feasible forms of implicit rationing that can occur with certain kinds of private financing. Implicit rationing

can occur because patients place a high degree of reliance on professional judgement. This reliance flows from the high degree of information asymmetry present in health care. Most obviously, implicit rationing can occur in a private financing context if the third party payers, namely insurance companies, employ rationing criteria which health-care professionals do not effectively communicate to patients (or regulators or other policy-makers). There is evidence that this kind of rationing has become increasingly common in the United States as insurance companies attempt to hold down costs.

4. **Private Financing-Explicit Rationing Criteria** Beyond the obvious rationing standard imposed by willingness-to-pay, explicit rationing in a market context can be associated with specific treatment limitations that insurers mandate in their plans. Most people in the private market for health care will wish to purchase health insurance rather than purchase health care in the "spot" market. Hence, formal limitations on scope of coverage are common in privately-financed insurance markets as well as public ones. Of course, it is the explicit rationing that the market imposes which has meant that no developed country relies exclusively on the market to finance health care, even where they rely heavily on private provision.

5. **Mixed Private and Public Financing** Several commentators predict that Canada will move increasingly to a more mixed system: "If the fiscal crunch intensifies, it would be surprising if several provinces did not take a closer look at the way in which the Europeans bring private sector funding into the core areas of medical and hospital services" (Courchene, 1994:180). As Besley and Gouveia (1994) point out, a mixed public and private financed system can be thought of as presenting health-care consumers with a sequential, or two-stage, decision problem. In their simple model, consumers first vote for some level of public provision, and second, they take this level of public provision as given, and decide their level of participation in the private market. A comprehensive assessment of the potential consequences of mixed financing systems is provided in a later chapter. This is a particularly complex and difficult topic because it raises both predictive and normative issues. Many Canadians fear that an increase in private financing will lead to decreases in quality in the public system *and* decreased political support for the public system.

CHAPTER THREE

Underlying Objectives In Rationing Health Care

Choosing among alternative criteria to ration health-care resources inevitably embodies value judgments about the social goals being pursued by the policymaker. Any socially acceptable rationing scheme must be consistent with the underlying values of society. In the preceding section, source-of-financing and explicit versus implicit rationing rules were described. In this section, broad potential objectives against which various health-care rationing schemes can be evaluated are outlined.[1]

Libertarianism

This position essentially holds that individuals are not *entitled* to any given level of health care and physicians are not *obliged* to provide any level of service to patients. Rather, transactions involving health-care resources should take place in private markets with little or no government mandating of the scope and nature of the transactions. This view would suggest that both the financing and delivery of health care should be private and that the criteria should be purely market-based; that is, what is profitable to produce as health care is what should be produced. The rationale for the libertarian position is that compulsion of individuals by the state is morally repugnant. It is buttressed by a view that the market system is an efficient way to organize transactions — basically there are no "market failures" or that government intervention almost always makes the resulting outcome less desirable. Thus, reliance upon non-market criteria will lead to reduced efficiency and economic welfare.

Critics of the libertarian position argue that private markets in health care are highly likely to be inefficient, so that government intervention could well improve efficiency. Moreover, many take a different position on the morality of making individual rights superior to social rights. Suffice to say that virtually no participant in the health-care debate (economist or non-economist) supports the libertarian position.

Utilitarianism and Cost/Benefit Analysis

This philosophical position holds that the social benefits and costs of alternative courses of action should be identified and evaluated. The plan that maximizes the benefit-cost ratio or net social benefits should be chosen.[2] As a practical matter, the utilitarian approach emphasizes

33

efficiency considerations in its choice of allocative rules. However, it does not assume that market-dictated allocation patterns will necessarily be efficient. Cost-benefit analysis in one guise or another has featured prominently in outcomes-based approaches to prioritizing health-care procedures; however, it continues to be subject to the broad criticism that it fails to address distributional issues explicitly, as well as to narrower criticisms surrounding the difficulties of identifying meaningful measures of benefit.[3] In a later section, we shall argue that utilitarianism underlies most of the explicit rationing criteria that are emerging in different countries and that distributional considerations can be incorporated into such an approach.

Many health-care experts have proposed what might be called a pragmatic approach to the allocation of health-care resources. Their proposals are not necessarily derived from any clearly defined philosophical position, although they appear to be primarily consistent with utilitarianism. However, in some proposals there are also elements of Rawlsianism and egalitarianism. Pragmatism is also closely related in spirit to incremental decision-making rules in situations of "bounded rationality". Such rules are associated with the contributions of Simon and Cyert and March to the administration theory literature (Simon, 1957; Cyert and March, 1963). The procedural rules recommended by Evans *et. al.* (1994) in this regard might be seen as an application of incremental (or sequential) decision-making under conditions of imperfect information.

Evans and his colleagues propose a sequential evaluation procedure for determining which medical procedures should be publicly-funded. They suggest that the evaluation be applied first to newly proposed procedures and then, perhaps, to established procedures. A procedure can be "rejected" for funding if it fails at any stage of the evaluation process. The first stage involves addressing the question: is the procedure in question "really" health care? The next stage addresses the question: does the procedure "work"? The third addresses the question: is the procedure "necessary"? The fourth addresses the question: "is there a "better" way of achieving the same results? In effect, Evans and his colleagues propose a sequential decision-making approach designed to eliminate procedures which either have no expected medical benefits, or benefits that are small relative to their costs, as well as procedures that are not cost-effective.

Eliminating procedures that have no medical benefits or that are not cost-effective unequivocally contributes to improved efficiency (assuming that consumers are relatively well-informed and rational). At the same time, no significant adverse distributional consequences need be considered if a procedure has no medical benefits for any patient. Patients are not disadvantaged in any meaningful way if the procedure is withheld from them. Similarly, if an equally effective, but cheaper, treatment is substituted for any given procedure, the patient is not worse off. As will be described in a subsequent section, utilization research, practice guidelines and technology assessment can sometimes lead to these kinds of "rationing". On the other hand, eliminating procedures that have some benefits, albeit small, relative to costs may have significant distributional consequences at the same time as it improves allocative efficiency. As an example, there is a growing body of opinion that testing for and treating prostate cancer may have small benefits relative to costs; however, reducing or eliminating prostate cancer diagnostic testing and treatment protocols while maintaining or expanding such activities for breast cancer violates a principle of strictly equal access to health care across gender. Given these problems, eliminating procedures that have no medical benefits or that are cost-ineffective is a relatively uncontroversial rationing rule, while eliminating procedures which have some benefits for some patients — although few benefits in aggregate — is more controversial.[4] In particular, if some procedures have expected benefits which exceed expected costs but governments wish to limit the amount of expenditures made on health care, criteria for prioritizing those procedures will be required. In this case, a strict ranking by cost-effectiveness may conflict with equity considerations. .

Application of a sequential decision-making procedure requires extensive and reliable clinical information that, at a minimum, identifies procedures that are unlikely to improve the health status of most patients or which cost more than other procedures providing equivalent results. In the next chapter, the available evidence bearing on the issue of whether this is likely to be a relatively large or relatively small set of medical procedures is reviewed. At this point, it is merely noted that the necessary "outcomes-based" clinical testing is at an early stage and that results seem quite sensitive to the characteristics of patients and other attributes of the clinical setting. This is likely to increase concerns about equity. Institutional arrangements in the health-care sector may also be important in terms of providing incentives to eliminate procedures that have no medical benefits or that are cost-ineffective. In particular, to the extent that incentives differ depending upon the extent of private versus public funding of health care, any evaluation of private financing of health care as a supplement to public funding should pay attention to this issue.

In summary, the application of utilitarian (benefit-cost) rules to allocate health-care resources presents even greater analytical challenges than does the identification and assessment of non-beneficial or cost-ineffective procedures. For one thing, more stringent demands are placed on getting right the estimates of the associated benefits and costs, since the analyst must weigh the estimates of one against the other, as well as the estimate of the net benefits of one procedure against those of other procedures. For another, the decision to fund or not fund procedures with non-trivial medical benefits implies potentially significant changes in the distribution of health-care resources across different groups in society. Thus, the analyst must also be able to identify the groups primarily affected by different procedures in order to evaluate the "fairness" of alternative patterns of funding. Given the potential importance of benefit/cost analysis as a decision-rule in the allocation of health-care resources, we offer a detailed evaluation of the technique as it applies to health-care policy in the next section.

Rawlsianism and Maximin Analysis

This position derives from John Rawls' well-known theory of justice (Rawls, 1971). It essentially implies that the goal of a health policy, or any other social welfare program, should not be to maximize aggregate net benefits or even the "average citizen's" welfare but should maximize the position of certain least well-off members of society, that is, a maximin criterion. Consistent with this view, policies which improve the welfare of others can be just if they do so as a consequence of maximizing the position of the least well-off. Very few participants in the health-care debate have taken a "pure" Rawlsian position, although many explicitly acknowledge the importance of protecting the access of poor people to health-care resources. Indeed, many would argue that policies which promise to increase overall net social benefits are undesirable if they reduce the access that the poor have to health care. Others, albeit a smaller number, argue that policies improving efficiency are undesirable if they improve access of the wealthy to health care more than they improve the access of the poor, notwithstanding that both groups may be absolutely better off.

Although few have adapted a pure Rawlsian perspective, many adopt what is, in practice, a neo-Rawlsian perspective. This perspective is as follows. If one were to look at the provision of health care from behind a "veil of ignorance" (that is, in a state where one did not know what one's health state or income would be), many would opt for a system with some degree of redistribution. The thought of ourselves (and our families) possibly being without any access to health care would be unappealing. If one finds the idea of a veil of ignorance normatively attractive, a degree of universal health care can be thought of as efficient as well as equitable.

Behind the veil, it is rational (and efficient) to design in *some* health care for everyone provided members of the society are risk averse. However, it is unlikely that even behind a veil of ignorance most would demand *equal* health care for everyone.

Egalitarianism

Egalitarianism essentially holds that the moral criterion for the evaluation of health-care policy alternatives should be the equalization of individual net benefits. That is, all individuals should receive the same net benefits from the health-care system. A somewhat less rigid expression of the egalitarian position holds that health-care policy should equalize the opportunities for individuals to benefit from health care. The latter criterion can clearly lead to much different allocation patterns than the former. In particular, individuals can experience vastly different health-care outcomes given equal opportunities to access health-care resources. Practical considerations, for example, it is easier to measure access across individuals than net benefits, predispose most participants concerned about distributional issues to focus on equality of opportunities (or access) rather than equality of outcomes.[5] Indeed, equality of access is the philosophical bedrock of the Canadian health-care system, according to the rhetoric of the federal government.

Most egalitarian-oriented policy analysts and policy-makers would propose some complex blend of two or more of the broad criteria outlined above. In particular, most would acknowledge that efficiency and equity are important broad criteria guiding the allocation of health-care resources. For example, at the extreme, few would argue for the uncompromised pursuit of "equality of opportunity" if it jeopardizes the ability of the health-care system to maintain and improve the health status of broad segments of the population, say because there are insufficient funds or skilled resources to perform a range of beneficial treatments and procedures.

Other Principles

A number of other principles for allocating health-care resources have been suggested. A number of contributors to the health-care debate suggest that age should be used more explicitly as a determinant of rationing. In particular, Callahan (1987) argues that it is in society's interest to dedicate fewer resources to health care supplied to the elderly, that is, those over 65, although he offers no precise allocation rules to determine which procedures should be offered (and to whom) and which

37

should not. Others stress the inappropriateness of spending large sums of money on "end-of-life" procedures that, at best, perpetuate longevity without improving the patient's "quality-of-life". In this latter form, the argument to reduce funding of health care for the elderly reflects a utilitarian perspective, that is, maximize net quality-of-life adjusted benefits of health-care expenditures, whereas Callahan argues his position from an ethical perspective; that is, it is fundamentally unethical for the elderly to disadvantage younger (and future) generations by preempting resources unduly merely to increase longevity.[6]

There is little doubt that the cost of the publicly-funded system would be substantially reduced if the scope and magnitude of coverage for the elderly were significantly reduced. As already described, the elderly (those over 65) are generally high-cost users of medical services. They are more likely to have chronic medical problems which require repeated admissions to the hospital. They are also more likely to have debilitating illnesses that last for relatively long periods of time (Blank, 1988).

Analysts who argue for criteria that emphasize anticipated length-of-life increments as the basis for rationing should recognize that individuals will rationally incorporate expectations about how they will be treated in their old age by the Medicare system in determining how much financial (and other) support they will give that system in their younger years. For many, support for the Medicare system during their earlier, healthier years is a contribution to a "medical savings plan" to be drawn upon in later years. Any significant denial of benefits based primarily upon age would undermine the willingness of many individuals, particularly those who are currently healthy and with above-average incomes, to support Medicare through their taxes.

Several other contributors argue that individuals must accept responsibility for health-care expense burdens that are the result of "life-style choices" such as smoking, drinking, drug-use and so forth. They argue that reduced public funding for procedures that address the medical consequences of life-style choices is "fair", in that it encourages individuals to reduce the funding burdens they place on the system. In other words, it reduces "moral hazard".[7] Critics of this view point out that it is difficult in many cases to identify when a medical condition is the result of life style choice rather than genetics or other environmental contributants. Application of this "moral hazard" rule would only be fair if there is a reliable and significant link between life style choice and health status. Accumulating evidence that individuals may be genetically predisposed to pathologies such as alcoholism is relevant and suggestive of the complexity surrounding this issue. Other critics argue that it is unfair to single out some life style choices for implicit censure and not others. For example, should upper-income individuals in high stress occupations be eligible for procedures dealing with the consequences of stress and a sedentary lifestyle, while alcoholics are denied procedures to address their health problems? If almost any life style choice is at least a partial contributor to most health problems, wouldn't the consistent application of a moral hazard-based rule for public funding ultimately eliminate most procedures from the acceptable set?

CHAPTER FOUR

Mechanisms For Explicitly Rationing Health

In the framework presented earlier, it was noted that if government wished to move from implicit rationing criteria to explicit rationing criteria, there were a number of alternative mechanisms for doing so. The first two of these mechanisms related to committee ranking methods. The major focus of this section is on cost-effectiveness rankings. Other committee allocation methods are also discussed because, for various reasons, the emerging case studies suggest that a "pure" cost-benefit or cost-effectiveness ranking system is (not yet) feasible. It is also useful to discuss related issues such as utilization rate studies, geographic, and institutional variation studies, and clinical practice guidelines.[1] These are discussed initially.

Utilization Research (UR) and Clinical Practice Guidelines

The simplest method of improving cost-effectiveness is to hold constant effectiveness and reduce cost. This can sometimes be done by substituting a lower cost component or reducing utilization of some input. *Prima facie* evidence of the potential for such cost reduction is often suggested by geographic and institutional variations in practice and utilization rates. Theoretically, of course, such analyses might be as likely to identify underutilization of more costly inputs as overutilization. But "although UR could be used to detect underutilization, the failure to provide necessary services, as well as to identify overutilization, typically it is restricted to the latter" (Restuccia, 1995:254). While *per se* such variations do not signify overutilization, they are suggestive evidence of overutilization when there are few differences in health status or other relevant differences in the population (Paccaud and Guillain, 1994; Wennberg, 1984; Chassin *et. al.*, 1987; Wennberg, 1987). For example, one recent study of U.S. medicare usage found that "although there is high overall variation, some of the categories of service demonstrate extreme variation. Previous research suggests that certain of the services, diagnostic imaging and testing for example, are more susceptible to inappropriate use..." (Miller, Holahan, and Welch, 1995). A recent Canadian example of practice variation analysis has been conducted by the Institute for Clinical Evaluative Sciences in Ontario which has found enormous variations from county to county and from region to region (Naylor, Anderson, and Goel, 1994).

A number of methodologies have been developed over the last decade to conduct utilization research. These include AEP (Appropriateness Evaluation Protocol), ISD criteria (intensity-of-service criteria), MRS (the Medical Review System), *Quality* FIRST, and MCAP (the Managed Care Appropriateness Protocol) (Dubois, 1991; Paccaud and Guillain, 1994; Restuccia, 1995). The MCAP criteria, for example, are based on "relevant medical literature, input from AEP users, analysis of the health care environment, application of draft criteria to medical records, and the medical expertise of clinicians practicing in managed care settings..." (Restuccia, 1995:256). As one would expect, the main challenge has been in defining what is appropriate utilization. An important area of research has been on inter-rater reliability in defining appropriate utilization. Different experts may disagree on what is appropriate treatment. Unless there is a high degree of agreement among these expert-raters, the validity of UR will be uncertain. The evidence suggests that inter-rater reliability is an important issue and that with newer instruments reliability has steadily improved (Dubois, 1991; Restuccia, 1995).

The most common way to lower cost that has been identified in health care is the reduction or elimination of hospitalization (Donabedian, 1982; Wickizer, 1990). Perhaps the most prominent Canadian example of the use of UR has occurred in Saskatchewan. Using ISD criteria, it was found that only about 45 percent of adult hospitalization was appropriate (Lewis, 1995:326). There has also been a great deal of effort in Europe to develop Pan-European hospital utilization criteria (Liberati, Apolone, Lang, and Lorenzo, 1995).

Variation analysis and UR have provided much of the stimulation for the development of clinical practice guidelines: "Guidelines contain advice on how to manage particular clinical problems with the intention of reducing the considerable variability which seems to characterize the treatment of most diseases" (Armstrong, Fry, and Armstrong, 1994:199). Practice guidelines actually guide physicians in making clinical decisions; they are "systematically developed statements to assist practitioner and patient decisions about appropriate health care for specific clinical circumstances" (Lohr, 1994:18). The U.S. Institute of Medicine has developed eight criteria for guidelines. The most important is validity, which is based on the strength of the evidence and the health and cost outcomes. Other criteria are reliability/reproducibility, clinical applicability, clinical flexibility (the identification of exceptions), clarity, multidisciplinary process, scheduled review and meticulous documentation (Field and Lohr, 1992:Table 1-1).

In Canada, the development of clinical guidelines, while in its infancy, is taking place within the context of the accommodation between the medical profession and the state. A number of provinces have developed joint profession-government bodies to develop clinical guidelines, although the fiscal sanctions associated with the guidelines vary considerably. In Saskatchewan, for example, guidelines on thyroid tests issued by the Health Services Utilization and Research Commission resulted in a reduction in overall volume of over 30 percent and a marked drop (65 to 79 percent) in the ordering of certain tests in circumstances in which the guidelines suggested they were not indicated. In British Columbia, an undertaking to develop clinical guidelines backed by legislation and fiscal sanctions formed the centerpiece of an agreement negotiated between the BC Medical Association and the BC government in August 1993. In Ontario, an Institute for Clinical Evaluative Sciences has been established under the aegis of a Joint Management Committee of the Ontario Medical Association and the provincial government (Tuohy, 1995:24).

The State of the Art in CBA, CEA, and CUA

There are essentially three formal procedures which can be used to estimate the net social value of health treatment outcomes: cost-benefit analysis (CBA), cost-effectiveness analysis (CEA), and cost-utility analysis (CUA). Cost-benefit analysis is the most comprehensive form of analysis; it attempts to measure all the social costs and benefits of a particular program or policy. It is firmly based in utilitarianism. A dollar valuation is placed on lives saved (Viscusi, 1993; Jones-Lee, 1989). In its pure form, benefits or costs accruing to different income groups are treated equally (in other words the marginal utility of income is considered to be constant and equal for all individuals) and all costs — not just budgetary costs — are included. CBA not only produces a ranking of alternative programs it also provides a decision rule for deciding whether a program is socially worthwhile. CBA is relatively rare in health care, for reasons that will be discussed below. Given the rarity of CBA in health care, it is not discussed at length.

Cost-effectiveness analysis and cost-utility analysis are commonly used alternatives to CBA in health care.[2] These methods are potentially useful when analysts seek efficient policies but face constraints that prevent them from doing CBA. Three analytical constraints are common. First, analysts may be unwilling or unable to monetize the most important policy impact. This constraint arises most frequently in the evaluation of alternative policies that save lives: many people are willing to predict the number of lives saved by alternative programs, but are unwilling to place a dollar value on the lives saved. This constraint appears to be particularly prevalent in health care. The second constraint arises when analysts recognize that a particular effectiveness measure does not capture all of the social benefits of each alternative, and some of these other social benefits are difficult to monetize. In using CBA, analysts face the burden of monetizing all impacts. If the effectiveness measure captures "most" of the benefits, it may be reasonable for analysts to use CEA to avoid the burden of conducting a comprehensive CBA. This is particularly true for health care, where increased quantity and quality of life are often the dominant types of benefits. The third constraint arises when analysts deal with intermediate outputs whose linkage to preferences is not clear. For example, the exact contribution of different levels of hospital-bed utilization to overall health is often unclear. In such situations, CBA is not possible, but CEA may give useful information concerning relative efficiency. For all these reasons CEA (and CUA, to be described below) have tended to dominate in health-care evaluation. Therefore, most academic debate has centered around how CEA and CUA should actually be used in the health arena.

In some circumstances the rankings of alternatives produced by CEA and CBA will be identical.[3] As mentioned above, however, CBA not only produces a ranking of alternatives, it also reveals whether the highest ranked, or any of the other alternatives, increase efficiency. CEA produces a ranking, but does not provide explicit information about whether there would be positive net social benefits associated with any of the alternatives being considered. However, in those circumstances where alternatives are mutually exclusive, and the status quo is among the alternatives (sharing similar scale and patterns of costs and benefits), then CEA does select the most efficient policy.

In almost all situations, the effectiveness measure selected by analysts (or decision makers) for use in CEA does not correspond to social benefits as measured in CBA, which are ultimately based on the willingness-to-pay of individuals. One can, however, reasonably infer that in many circumstances individuals would demonstrate willingness-to-pay for incremental units of "effectiveness" such as "lives saved". In other circumstances the inference is more tenuous. For example, "number of addicts treated" may or may not be an approximate measure for such benefits as reductions in street crime and the other negative externalities of drug abuse (Drummond, Stoddart, and Torrance, 1987).

As discussed above, CEA does not monetize benefits. Thus, it inevitably involves two different metrics: cost in dollars and an effectiveness measure — for example, lives saved, or children vaccinated. Because one cannot add or subtract non-commensurable metrics, one cannot obtain a single measure of net social benefits from the two metrics. One can only compute the ratio of the two measures as a basis for ranking alternative policies. This can be done in one of two ways. First, one can measure cost-effectiveness in terms of cost per unit of outcome effectiveness; for example, cost per life saved. To compute this, one takes the ratio of the budgetary cost of each alternative to the effectiveness (or benefit) of that alternative. This ratio can be thought of as the average cost per unit of effectiveness. The most cost-effective project has the lowest average cost per unit of effectiveness. Second, cost-effectiveness can be calculated as the ratio of the outcome effectiveness units per unit of budgetary cost. This ratio can be thought of as the average effectiveness per unit of cost. The most cost-effective project has the highest average effectiveness per unit of cost.

Cost-utility analysis, CUA, also relates budgetary costs to a single effectiveness measure, but this measure is a construct made up of several (usually two) effectiveness categories. For example, the benefit measure may be quality-adjusted life-years (QALYs). QALYs are concerned with bringing together both mortality and morbidity aspects of health into a single measure. As an example, respondents might be asked: "Would you prefer 10 years in state X or 20 years in state Y?" where state Y is a worse state of health than state X. If state X is taken to be perfect health and the respondent is indifferent between the two choices when the length of time in state Y is 15 years, then state Y is "valued" at two-thirds of perfect health and is therefore weighted as .67. If an individual can be moved from that state to perfect health for the 10-year period, then the QALYs gained by this amount are 3.3, that is, $10 - (1 - .67) \times 10$.[4] When estimating QALYs across a group of people, the QALY weight is normally taken as some weighted average of the population's values. Obviously taking averages across the population raises the risk of discounting or ignoring individual differences in preferences towards health.

The example cited above employs the "time trade-off" method for estimating QALYs. Other methods include the health rating method and the standard gamble method. The first of these scales differences between health states along a zero-one line, with perfect health and death being one and zero. Respondents are asked to place some intermediate health state, for example, a broken leg, on the line. If the point were, say, 0.9, then being in the state of "broken leg" involves a 10 percent loss of health.

With the standard gamble, probabilistic choices are involved: would an individual prefer the certainty of health state X (which is less than perfect) for 10 years followed by death, or some probability of perfect health for 10 years followed by death and one minus that probability of immediate death. When the individual is indifferent with a probability of

P, then that P represents the value of state X when perfect health equals one.[5]

If analysts use *either* additional years of life per dollar cost, *or* a quantitative index of improved quality of life per dollar cost, they are doing CEA. The rationale for CUA is that *both* the number of additional years *and* the quality of life during those years are important benefit categories. In CUA the (incremental) costs of alternative policies are compared to the health changes, usually measured in the QALYs that they produce. CUA is most useful when a trade-off must be made between quality of life (morbidity) and length of life (mortality). In principle, however, CUA could be used with any two distinct dimensions of health status. CUA can be thought of as a subset of CEA which employs a more complex effectiveness measure. The rationale for distinguishing CUA is that considerable analytical effort has gone into the specific issues relating to developing QALYs.

As QALYs involve two distinct variables — quality and quantity — CUA must designate how these variables are to be defined and combined. Consider, for example, three mutually exclusive alternative pre-natal programs. Under the status quo, no babies with a particular condition are born alive. Pre-natal alternative A will result in five babies being born alive per year, but with permanent, serious disabilities. Pre-natal alternative B will result in only two live births, but with only low levels of disability. Before the costs of these alternatives can be compared to their effectiveness, quantity and quality have to be made commensurate.

In order to develop QALYs, health economists have had to decide "who decides?". With one exception to be described below, the basic approach has been that the public, rather than the experts, should decide on most of the basic trade-offs, including the most basic trade-off: that between quantity and quality of life. Thus CUA is based primarily on a utilitarian framework. CUA requires, first, that different health states be specified, or defined.

Defining health status is complex. Descriptions of different health states are normally defined by CUA researchers in collaboration with clinicians familiar with variations in health — whether in relationship to particular diseases, injuries, and mental states, or to health in general. This reliance on experts is based on the assumption that neither the public nor potential treatment subjects are likely to have enough information and knowledge to formulate health state descriptions. Most often experts formulate descriptions of health for specific diseases or illnesses. George Torrance and his colleagues, however, have developed a comprehensive multi-dimensional health classification system with the following dimensions: physical function (mobility and physical activity); role function (ability to care for oneself); social-emotional function (emotional well-being and social activity), and "health problem" (including physical deformity) (Torrance, Boyle, and Horwood, 1982; Kind, Rosser, and Williams, 1982).

The second step is to determine how individuals compare and rank these health states; that is, to determine the "utility" they derive from the different health state descriptions. There are three common methods of deriving utilities as mentioned earlier: the health rating method, the time-trade-off method, and the standard gamble method. The methods vary in the extent to which they correspond to the economic concept of utility (Froberg and Kane, 1989).

There is one important note of caution in terms of health ratings. While the evidence suggests that respondents are reasonably accurate in determining rank order (that is, that health state A was preferable to health state B), there is evidence that they are not as confident in their estimates of rank distance (that is, *how much more* preferred health state A is to health state B) (Nord, 1991; Nord, 1993).

Not all issues related to QALYs are resolved (for an excellent review of these issues, see Loomes and McKenzie, [1989]). One problem is the issue of discounting additional years of life. The basic idea that individuals have positive discount rates is widely accepted, but there is considerable controversy over the theory, measurement and level of the appropriate discount rate (Gafni, 1995; Redelmeier, Heller, and Weinstein, 1994; Johannesson, Pliskin, and Weinstein, 1994). While many of these issues remain unresolved, it is problematic to discount costs but not to discount years. The reason is that it would always make sense to delay the health expenditure until next year because the cost-effectiveness ratio will improve (Keeler and Cretin, 1983). However, this is not a paradox because, as we have pointed out, cost-effectiveness does not ever reveal *per se* whether a procedure is worthwhile.

Consistent Use of CEA and CUA Methodology

Even though both CEA and CUA are used widely by analysts working in health, they are not applied consistently. There is great variation in practices such as: the specification of alternative policies, the justification of effectiveness measures, the inclusiveness of cost measures, and the discounting of effectiveness over time. Indeed, one recent review of the application of CEA and CUA to the evaluation of health policies found that approximately one-half of the studies examined were of less than adequate quality (Gerard, 1992:271). Other reviews have reached similar conclusions (Salkeld, Davey, and Arnolda, 1995).

Other issues also remain unresolved. Three seem of particular importance. First, the methodologies are essentially based upon asking individuals about their preferences, rather than relying on their revealed preferences; their actual behaviour. Therefore, these methods are potentially subject to many bias and calibration problems that arise when individuals are asked questions about complex valuations in unfamiliar contexts. Samples drawn from the general public, for example, are likely to be prone to hypotheticality problems (Hausman, 1993) — they simply have not thought very much about these kinds of issues. This problem can be ameliorated somewhat by providing detailed descriptions of the various health states and the expected changes in years of life. This assists respondents in thinking in cardinal terms, as against ordinal terms, about their preferences (see above). Second, in practice convenience samples, rather than random samples, are often drawn from the general population. On the other hand, respondents who are potential treatment candidates because they are already ill may have incentives to exaggerate the "utility" they would receive from better health states. Third, either type of sample may be subject to framing effects inherent in the questionnaire approach.[6]

In spite of all these caveats, there is evidence that different samples — whether the general public, potential treatment candidates, or physicians, as well as different sexes, ages and races — do not vary much in their responses, either in terms of ranking health states or making trade-offs (Sackett and Torrance, 1978). This suggests that a relative consensus could be reached in ranking alternative treatments. On the other hand, different utility derivation techniques produce different weightings. One recent survey, for example, found that six different methods to assess preferences did not correlate that well (Hornberger, Redelmeier, and Peterson, 1992). Our overall assessment is that there is some degree of consensus on both methodological format and remaining core methodological questions.

Can CBAs, CEAs and CUAs be Used to Allocate Health-care Resources?

The answer to this question depends upon a number of factors including: (1) the number and quality of studies; (2) the purpose for which the studies are used, and (3) the ability of decision makers to use the studies.

1. **Number and Quality of Studies** The first question is whether there are sufficient studies emerging to provide reliable policy guidance to decision makers who must rank procedures. In social science such

rankings are often referred to as "league tables". This issue is central for two reasons. First, unless there are a large number of studies covering the *same* medical intervention, there can be little confidence in external validity. Second, unless there are studies covering a wide range of *different* medical interventions (in other words, comprehensiveness) there can be little hope that decision makers can actually use such studies to rank, prioritize or ration health-care resources. To continue with the league table metaphor, if one doesn't know the wins and losses of most of the teams, the league rankings will not tell one much about which are the good and bad teams overall. A prerequisite for economic analysis of medical procedures is evidence of clinical or medical impact. This is sometimes described as technology assessment. As Mosteller and Frazier (1995:19) point out, "We need technology assessment because medical innovations often fail to deliver the hoped-for benefits".

"Randomized control trials" potentially provide the most appropriate framework for conducting CBA, CEA and CUA. In randomized control trials, subjects are randomly assigned to either a treatment group or a control group. Such an experimental procedure can provide the ideal evidence for *ex post* CBA or CEA, which can then be used for *ex ante* policy purposes (Boardman, Mallery and Vining, 1994). Almost all *new* potential treatments are now subject to randomized trials. There is, however, no guarantee that medical treatments that are "standard" and have been in place for a long period of time have been subject to such an experimental design. Between 1966 and 1968 there were at least fifty thousand "medical" trials (Adams *et. al.*, 1992). However, only 0.2 percent of studies during that time included economic analysis (Adams *et. al.*, 1992:234). Additionally, even most of those studies that did include some attempt at economic analysis were not comprehensive and, indeed, for many of these studies it was impossible to determine the economic perspective (that is, there was no clear perspective on standing, or "who counts", Whittington and McCrae, 1986). There has been, however, some improvement in the inclusion of economic analysis in randomized trials over time. This is consistent with other evidence that economic studies have become more numerous since 1988 (Salkeld, Davey, and Arnolda, 1995). Although it is not clear whether the rate of growth of such studies is increasing, it seems clear that some disease areas are much more popular for study than others, and that some important disease areas have not been studied at all, at least in some jurisdictions (Gerard, 1993:118). Most clinical trials *could* include appropriate socio-economic analysis if the correct combination of incentives and expertise were present. Therefore, decision makers *can* be potentially provided with CEAs and CUAs to help allocate scarce health resources in a comprehensive manner. Is this taking place?

2.   **The Aggregation of CEA and CUA Studies**   It is important to recognize that CEA and CUA can be used in two different ways: to compare mutually exclusive alternative treatments (different ways of treating the same problem) or as "league tables" to compare *across* procedures that are not mutually exclusive. The former use is *relatively* uncontroversial, since it, in principle, results in no reduction of overall levels of care provided. However, if CEA and CUA are used to allocate resources across different health-care "conditions", league tables that comprehensively rank non-mutually exclusive treatments are required.

Comparisons of mutually exclusive projects inherently control for some of the differences in the measurement of cost and effectiveness, since they are essentially dealing with the same clinical situation. There can be no such presumption when comparing studies across different authors, using different data, and somewhat different methodologies. Different studies may measure costs differently, they may omit different costs, they may have different definitions of social benefits, and they may differ considerably in scale. These problems apply even more to CUA than CEA studies, especially because different methodologies are used to calculate QALYs and, as discussed earlier, alternative QALY methodologies do not necessarily produce identical or even consistent results.

A review of the health economics and health policy literature suggests that there *are* a large number of studies emerging (particularly CUA studies), many of which adopt a multi-country perspective. Table 4.1 summarizes some of the studies performed in the last decade on the value of three medical interventions: cholesterol-lowering interventions, vaccination programs and hypertension. The table suggests that CEAs and CUAs, at least for certain kinds of medical interventions, are becoming more common. However, one recent review concluded that even in 1995, "gathering all of the clinical trials in a field, organizing them according to topic, and carrying out research synthesis on each question having adequate randomized clinical trials has been done only for obstetrics" (Mosteller and Frazier, 1995:25). The same authors, however, point out that the situation can be expected to improve in the near future: "there is a substantial movement, led by Iain Chalmers of the UK Cochrane Centre, to organize the results of all kinds of studies... when completed, the findings will be invaluable..." (Mosteller and Frazier, 1995:247). Similar efforts are underway in North America, as exemplified by "Five Hundred Life-Saving Interventions and their Cost-Effectiveness" (Tengs *et. al.*, 1995).

Table 4.1

Cite	Health Issue
Kinosian and Eisenberg (1988)	Cholesterol levels
Martens, Ruttens and Erkelens et. al. (1989)	Cholesterol levels
Shulman, Kinosian, Jacobson et. al. (1990)	Cholesterol levels
Kristiansen, Eggen and Thelle (1991)	Cholesterol levels
Krahnz and Detsky (1993)	Hepatitis B vaccination
Antonanzas, Garuz, Anton, Truxet, Navas and Salleras (1995)	Hepatitis B vaccination
Bloom, Hillman, Fendrick and Schwartz (1993)	Hepatitis B vaccination
Arevalo and Washington (1988)	Hepatitis B vaccination
Demicheli and Jefferson (1992)	Hepatitis B vaccination
Johannesson and Jonsson (1991)	Hypertension
Kowachi and Malcolm (1991)	Hypertension
Edelson et. al. (1990)	Hypertension

Finally, if league table rankings include studies from different jurisdictions, they increase the risk of comparing populations with different "baseline" conditions. To take an extreme example, while a malaria abatement program in Africa may show a low cost per QALY, this result cannot be extrapolated to Norway. More subtly, different population groups are subject to different genetic problems, and different incidence rates which can qualify the outcomes of evaluation studies. For example, the cost-effectiveness of hypertension treatment varies widely by age, sex and risk factors (Johannesson and Jonsson, 1991). This is often described as variable opportunity costs across jurisdictions, but since benefits are usually simply avoided costs, this problem applies to effectiveness as much as costs. Ideally, therefore, league tables should be based on studies from the same, or very similar jurisdictions (countries).[7]

Karen Gerard's caution on the use of league tables is appropriate:

> As more and more studies were read in the course of the investigation, it became striking how many not only placed their results in some standard QALY league table but also purported to present their results as 'favourable'. It is unlikely to be the case that all of these studies can have 'favourable' results (Gerard, 1992:274).

Of course, it is only possible for all authors to conclude that results are "favorable" because there is no explicit cut-off in CEA or CUA. As will be discussed further below, there are only two alternative ways of using such league tables to allocate resources at the margin: either heuristically by picking some arbitrary cut-off point or explicitly by putting a dollar value on lives saved and/or quality improvements in life. This, of course, requires that CEA and CUA become more like CBA. Put in other words, without explicitly valuing human lives and/or quality improvements in life, no evaluation technique can "tell" the policymaker how much to spend on health care, in total. The spending cut-off point remains essentially a political decision.

3. **The Ability of Decision Makers to Use CEA, CUA and Related Studies** A third critical issue is whether decision makers have the ability to understand the relevant studies along with the political will to utilize them. In addressing these questions we review the preliminary evidence from a number of countries, including the United Kingdom, Australia, New Zealand, the United States and Canada.

The major change that has occurred in the last twenty years is that the number of *independently-produced* analyses have increased steadily since the 1960s. However, the evidence has also suggested that, over most of the period, the influence of economic evaluations has not, as yet, been great (Drummond, Brandt, Luce, and Rovira (1993). We review the evidence on use on a country-by-country basis.

In the United Kingdom, the Department of Health recently published the first Register of Cost-Effectiveness Studies (RCES) (DOH, 1994). The RCES produced in 1994 contained assessments of 147 economic valuations. The results, after considerable debate, were not presented in a league table format (Mason, Drummond, and Torrance, 1993; Drummond, Mason, and Torrance, 1993). Some critics have claimed that even a simple presentation of data would do more harm than good (Birch and Gafni, 1994). As explained above, CEA only examines one (or in the case of CUA, two) outcome categories and are also variable in quality. They are, therefore, difficult to compare. For example, a simple compilation of CEAs from a variety of locales ignores local opportunity costs. Nevertheless, many commentators argue that league tables are valuable in this context and that the Register itself generates improvements in the comparison process:

> One important by-product of the work on RCES has been the specification of a template for the reporting of economic evaluations. In addition, more thought has been given to the ways in which the cost-effectiveness of a given intervention varies from setting to setting and to elements of standardization on the international

level that might assist decision makers in interpreting the results of published studies (Drummond, Mason, and Torrance, 1995:235).

In the United Kingdom, probably the most well-known league table has been the one produced by Alan Maynard (1991). His table suggests that cost per QALY varied from £220 for cholesterol testing and diet therapy for adults between 40 and 69 to £126,290 for erythropoietin treatment for anemia in dialysis patients. How influential have such league tables been in influencing National Health Services purchasers? Thus far, not very (Klein, 1994). This is not surprising at this point. It reflects the fact that many kinds of procedures have still not been subject to CEA, CUA or CBA evaluation (Smith, 1992) and even finding out which services are currently being offered requires considerable research.

In the United States, experience with CEA and CUA is moving on a number of fronts. Most of the experience is in the public sector. However, the private sector (particularly HMOs and other health alliances) is increasingly utilizing clinical data in cost-effectiveness evaluations (Stodghill, 1995). We first consider the Federal level and then the experience at the State level, most importantly Oregon.

The U.S. government announced in 1991 that it was beginning to develop a league table for regulations that would attempt to reduce health and safety risks.

> "The approach will use cost-effectiveness analysis across a wide variety of regulatory programs, all aimed at reducing health and safety risks faced by members of society, to identify those activities that are most cost-effective, for example, that save lives or prevent illnesses/injuries at the lowest cost" (Morrall, 1992:17).

Eleven pilot programs were initially selected for testing, including immunization programs and seafood safety regulation. At the moment comparisons are only being made within program areas, although there are plans to broaden the comparisons (Morrall, 1992). Much of this effort is being carried out by the Panel on Cost-Effectiveness in Medicine and Health (Hadorn, 1996).

In 1992, Congress stipulated that the Agency for Health Care Policy and Research should include economic importance in its own criteria for health technology assessment. This is likely to have a major impact on which technologies will be assessed (Phelps and Parente, 1990). The Office of Technology Assessment has recently concluded that "analyses that consider the costs and health effects of an intervention in a structured fashion can improve decisionmaking, and greater use of CEA in this context appears to be on the horizon" (OTA, 1994). Much of this evaluation activity has switched to the states: "State involvement in [technology assessment] is an emerging phenomenon, with most states engaging in a wide range of clinically oriented activities" (Mendelson, Abramson, and Rubin, 1995:95).

At the state level, Oregon has led in the development of explicit ranking mechanisms. The Oregon Health Services Commission had the primary responsibility for developing cost-effectiveness rankings for public health services (excluding long-term care, mental health and services for the disabled). The Oregon experiment has been controversial (for example, Daniels, 1991; La Puma and Lawlor, 1990; Nord, 1993; Kaplan, 1994). The Oregon Health Services Commission employed four procedures to assess Oregonians' valuations of health and health treatments: (1) values assessed in town meetings; (2) health state ratings; (3) subjective ratings about treatment effectiveness, and (4) Commissioners' assessments (Kaplan, 1994). Participants in the town meetings placed nine types of care into one of three categories: essential, very important, important. These types of care ranged from treatments of conditions where the treatment is likely to extend life by more than two years and improve quality to treatments expected to do neither (Kaplan, 1994). This procedure did not draw upon a random sample of Oregonians.

The ratings from the experiment formed the basis of an initial "trial run" ranking of 1,600 services by the Commission, which were never officially published. This cost-effectiveness league table was reviewed by the Office of Technology Assessment which concluded that many of the rankings were not appropriate (see below). Kaplan (1994:982) argues that the reason for most of the problems was simple: "The major difficulty with the initial Oregon exercise was the attempt to prioritize a large number of services in a relatively short period of time... the committee attempted to do several decades of work within the confinement of a few months... analysts sometimes take two to three years to thoroughly analyze the expected benefits of a single condition-treatment pair." Given this speed, it is not surprising that the procedure was subject to some of the problems already described: "Oregon did not take into account the costs incurred when a patient is not treated (costs were not net), did not compute costs relative to the next best alternative (costs were not 'marginal'), and did not consider the time at which the costs were incurred (costs were not 'discounted')" (Tengs *et. al.*, 1996:100). There were other technical problems. For example, it may well be that respondents were not able to effectively cardinalize their ratings of health states (Nord, 1993; Ubel, Loewenstein, Scanlon, and Kamlet, 1996).

The evidence suggests that rankings could be altered by interest group pressure. For example, medical support for very low birth weight infants was moved up the ranking even though there was evidence of no treatment effectiveness. The Commission sometimes altered rankings when they did not "look right". Additional problems were caused by the initial rejection of the ranking by the Federal government on the basis that the ratings discriminated against persons with disabilities. (Because the Oregon rankings would have revised Medicaid treatment policies they required a federal waiver; the rankings were finally approved and implemented in 1993.) The Federal objection to the rankings were clearly misconceived, but as a result of the Federal intervention the Oregon Commission was forced to drop the quality of life adjustment to life years (for details, see Kaplan, 1994). In 1994 the Oregon Plan went into effect with coverage extended to some 565 procedures, along with the cost of all prescriptions. In the end, some procedures such as cosmetic surgery, were left off the list on grounds that they were too marginal in medical value. It was decided that others, such as minor sprains, flu and mild food poisoning, could often be handled without a doctor. Still others, such as asthma and mononucleosis, are not covered unless there is a complicating factor (Appleby, 1994).

The most recent assessment of the Oregon experience is reasonably optimistic, concluding that "providers were surprisingly patient in learning to use the list"; that there was a "high degree of physician acceptance of the underlying concept and involvement by physicians in the development of the list"; that "since implementation, only one significant change has occurred", and finally, that "the concept of the list was relatively non-controversial within Oregon itself" (Thorne et. al., 1995:123). The major controversy is the extent to which the rankings reflect the ratio of effectiveness to costs as against other criteria. Tengs et. al. (1996) find that there is some correlation (Spearman rank-order correlation, +.30), but it is far from perfect. They attribute much of the problem to the "coarse" cost data available to the Oregon Health Services Commission and the failure to use appropriate discounting (Tengs et. al., 1996:106).

The Oregon rankings demonstrate that: (1) a convincing league table requires considerable analytic effort; (2) once any ranking is made explicit it becomes subject to "political" pressure to rerank; (3) it is possible to ration on the basis of rankings.

Australia has been a leader in the use of CUA. In 1987, amendments to the *National Health Act* required that the Pharmaceuticals Benefits Advisory Committee consider both costs and effectiveness in recommendations on new drugs to the Pharmaceutical Benefits Scheme. Once drugs are listed by the Scheme they are eligible for government subsidy (Salked, Davey, and Arnolda, 1995:112; Neumann and Johannesson, 1994a:209). These requirements became operational in January, 1993. The guidelines mandate that the economic analysis be based on a social perspective, that new drugs be compared to treatments that they are likely to replace, that analyses be presented both with and without indirect costs and that QALYs be used as the measure of effectiveness, but that intermediate indicators, such as changes in blood pressure levels, be used where appropriate (Neumann and Johannesson, 1994). The Advisory Committee has also been mandated to consider whether a given cost-effectiveness ratio should be considered "high" or "low" for decision making purposes.

Economic evaluation also appears to be gaining ground in other areas of health care in Australia, although it is still being held back by political factors, practical decision making constraints (short time frame, shortage of relevant studies, et cetera) and lack of user expertise (Ross, 1995:106). It has been argued that to make CEA more useful to Australian health decision makers two things are necessary: (1) a more concerted effort to ensure that decision makers understand the basic elements of CEA and CUA analysis, and (2) standardization of methodology and clear reporting of all elements of the study (Salked, Davey, and Arnolda, 1995:119).

In 1991, the New Zealand government proposed the establishment of a national committee to determine which "core" services would be provided through the public health system (Cumming, 1994). The committee was required to consider the distribution of services, their costs, their effectiveness and benefits, and to consult widely with health professionals and the public. This committee was to advise the four Regional Health Authorities who are now responsible for purchasing both primary care and hospital care. Although the previous allocation system clearly involved implicit rationing, there was considerable uneasiness over the concept of an explicit core (Bridgeport Group, 1992). The result has been broad guidelines, rather than specific rankings of treatments: "The core as exemplified by the service obligations is not that which was originally envisaged" (Cumming, 1994:49).[8]

Summary and Policy Conclusions on CEA and CUA Rankings

Explicit rationing criteria are still relatively rare in Canada. To date, few policy statements or guidelines have been issued by provinces to explain how priorities are set for treatments and procedures funded under Medicare and for deciding what procedures and treatments will be covered by the public insurance scheme. Concerns about waiting lists, potential age discrimination, exclusion from expensive treatments such as organ transplants based on other physical conditions such as Down's Syndrome and so forth have been relatively isolated in Canada. However, such concerns will certainly become more prominent in the future as the demand for health care grows relative to the supply financed by the Medicare system, since a much larger number of individuals are likely to see themselves as being systematically discriminated against by the selection (for treatment) process.

Some view a system based on implicit criteria as mitigating public tensions and concerns surrounding the use of scarce health-care resources. In particular, if "professional judgement" is accepted uncritically, the decisions of health-care administrators as to treatment priorities would go unchallenged by health-care users. However, social conflict related to concerns about discrimination and victimization is likely to be heightened by a regime in which priorities are implicitly set, since groups that are denied or delayed treatment can readily assume that the denials and delays are the result of discrimination. The use of explicit criteria such as QALYs would certainly not be free of lobbying pressures and other manifestations of social conflict. However, lobbying efforts are likely to be both more focused and more constrained, since grounds for complaint and appeal would be constrained by technical considerations.

The efficiency argument for adopting explicit rationing criteria is more compelling when the criteria emphasize economic considerations. Nevertheless, *any* set of explicit criteria has a unique efficiency advantage: it assists individuals to forecast the likelihood of receiving treatments and procedures under Medicare. Risk-averse individuals who project (or even know) that they will need a treatment that will not be covered can plan accordingly, including making arrangements for treatment outside the public insurance system (provided they are allowed to do so). Individual decision-making will be more rational if individuals have a more accurate assessment of the physical disabilities that they will probably need to cope with (and possibly succumb to) because of financial (or other) limitations on access to health care. One should perhaps not make too much of this point. After all, for many people, disease and disability are not readily forecastable. Nor are changes in health-care funding priorities. Nevertheless, clarity about public policy is usually seen as promoting more efficient decision-making, even under conditions of imperfect information.

It is much more difficult to recommend the specific set of explicit criteria that should be adopted. The imperative to "blend" efficiency and equity considerations in any set of criteria complicates the issue. However, it is not at all clear that a cost-effectiveness or cost-utility ranking procedure would systematically favour specific groups in such a way that horizontal or vertical equity would be violated. Specifically, there is no reason to believe that individuals in like circumstances would be treated differently, at least within jurisdictions that adopt similar "league tables" whether based on CEA criteria or broader criteria. This suggests that horizontal inequities are likely to be minimal. There is perhaps more reason to worry about vertical inequities. Some diseases, especially those influenced by lifestyle choices, will affect lower income groups more readily than higher income groups. At the other extreme, treatments that are more specific to the elderly, for example, heart bypass operations, may be more intensively consumed by above-average income patients, as such individuals live longer than lower income individuals. If league tables consistently ranked procedures dealing with certain lifestyle (or age) related pathologies systematically low (or high), systematic differences in effective access to health care would be created across income or other demographically distinct groups. However, based upon the evidence available to us, we have no reason to conclude that any such bias is likely to rise. That is, we have no reason to conclude that cost-effectiveness or cost-utility criteria would systematically favour pathologies of the rich relative to those of the poor or vice-versa. Hence, it seems possible to conclude that the latter criteria will improve allocative efficiency without necessarily offending any legitimate concerns about equity and fairness.

This discussion of theoretical developments in CEA/CUA and their (preliminary) use in a number of countries suggests some lessons for the development of Canadian policy. The good news is that the "state of the art" in CEA and CUA is no longer a major roadblock to their use in a policy context. While the use of CBA would be preferable because it generates an explicit cut-off point, there are not enough of these studies being generated. The bad news is that the lack of a comprehensive set of studies covering all health-relevant treatments in any given jurisdiction means that effective CEA/CUA league tables are only possible if certain conditions are met. First, it will be necessary to use studies from other jurisdictions that have similar baseline characteristics. In the Canadian context, this means a province would have to use CEA studies from other provinces, the United States and other developed countries with similar baseline profiles. Second, the body responsible for ranking treatments will have to commission studies in remaining missing areas. This also presents two problems. The first is obvious. These kinds of studies are costly and require considerable expertise (as we have seen, the evidence suggests quite high variability in the quality of studies; if studies are of poor quality the whole legitimacy of a ranking process will be undermined). The second problem is, however, likely to be more serious. To be convincing, such studies should be based on randomized trials; these often require extensive time frames — sometimes many years. Ranking commissions, even with extensive resources, are not going to be able to "conjure up" a comprehensive set of studies. If they try to do so, or pretend that they are doing so, they will be forced towards the Oregon solution, namely the de-emphasis of cost-effectiveness as the ranking criterion and the substitution of other criteria.

The expectation is that all developed countries will ultimately move aggressively to prioritize public and quasi-public health insurance expenditures on utilitarian-based criteria. For a variety of reasons, this will make it easier for smaller countries such as Canada to move in the same direction. Precisely how to do this is beyond the scope of this monograph's mandate. As well, implementation issues arise including: (1) should the use of utilitarian criteria be implemented immediately, albeit in a limited way, or should policymakers wait until a relatively comprehensive league table can be created? (2) what rationing criteria should be used over the foreseeable future when only limited reliable information is available to develop such a league table? While it is impractical to provide any extended defense of our position, we believe that a utilitarian criterion should be used whenever it can be reliably done so, even if it applies only to a subset of procedures. Such explicit criteria could facilitate a more efficient rationing of resources for that subset of treatments and procedures. While the potential efficiency gains are difficult to quantify, some very "bullish" forecasts have been made of the potential cost savings that can be gained simply by eliminating care that produces little or no benefit (for example, health-care expenditures could be cut as much as 30 percent; see Aaron, 1991). Efficiency gains on this magnitude would do much to ease financing pressures on the Medicare system to engage in more difficult rationing decisions.

The elimination of procedures that provide no medical benefits, or that provide equivalent benefits to other procedures but are more costly, are obvious and relatively uncontroversial sources of improved efficiency. However, many treatments are likely to provide some benefit (perhaps small) to some individuals and have no lower-cost alternatives. Once this is the case, decisions to fund or not fund require hard choices. This situation is likely to characterize many of the funding decisions that have to be made. For such cases, application of the utilitarian criterion requires cost-benefit analysis.

Implementation of any utilitarian-based rationing criteria requires: (1) the availability and dissemination of information; (2) the political will to adopt and use the criteria. Both are difficult. The production and dissemination of consistent information about medical efficacy is an international public good, and, therefore tends to be undersupplied (Pauly, 1996). This is true even with government doing most of the relevant funding. Efforts are being made to generate methodological standardization. For example, Spanish researchers have suggested standardization in terms of the selection of alternatives, the inclusion of direct versus indirect and intangible costs, methods for valuing costs, measures of health effects used, time horizon and discounting, the treatment of risk and uncertainty, sensitivity analysis and the presentation of results (OTA, 1994). The European Union is now engaged in an effort to develop such standards that will be adopted by "EU regulatory agencies, national administrations, and European multinational companies operating in the health care field with the final aim of harmonizing regulatory practices across EU countries (OTA, 1994).

Canada obviously should participate in these international efforts. Of course, there is more immediate potential in coordinating provincial efforts to pool and synthesize information about medical efficacy and related costs. In this regard, inter-provincial practice variation may "signal" the need for detailed cost-effectiveness studies.

The second requirement for implementation is the political will to implement utilitarian rationing criteria. Clearly in a system that is supplier-driven, has increasing budgets and is highly centralized, there will be little interest in utilitarian rationing criteria — or indeed any rationing criteria. However, Canada is moving to a health-care system that is more decentralized, has a better balance between suppliers and consumers, and has effectively capped budgets. Such an environment has much less room for fiscal illusion (that is, the illusion that someone else is paying for the system), or the belief that time is better spent on lobbying for more resources as opposed to trying to allocate existing dollars more effectively. Such an environment is more conducive to utilitarian criteria. But, as Oregon demonstrates, one can only be as utilitarian as the information allows. Thus, the two requirements go together.

CHAPTER FIVE

Mixing Public and Private Sources of Financing

It is obvious that any significant initiatives (whether implicit or explicit) to further ration publicly-financed health care will encourage increased demand for privately-financed health care. In this context, we have in mind a definition of private insurance that is narrower than is traditional in the literature. Namely, we exclude insurance plans that are administered by private insurers but that are mandatory and heavily regulated by the government. In a number of European countries, substantial portions of the population have insurance coverage through "private" insurers. However, coverage is usually mandatory and typically applied to employers, so that the coverage is essentially a payroll tax. Moreover, insurers are highly restricted in their scope to accept or reject members, as well as to include or exclude procedures and treatments for coverage (Glaser, 1991; Kirkman-Liff, 1994). As a practical matter, such systems are fundamentally tax-based, albeit indirectly so.

In the ensuing discussion, private insurance refers to payments to third-party insurers or out-of-pocket expenditures (self-insurance) that are entirely voluntary and only minimally regulated, if at all. It is certainly possible for increased private insurance to take a mandated and highly regulated form, either along European lines or along the lines proposed by President Clinton in his health care reform initiative. However, it is unclear why policymakers would choose to substitute highly regulated, mandatory private insurance for direct taxes as a means to finance health care, if the motivation for reducing government health-care expenditures is the reduction of the deadweight costs of government on the Canadian economy. In any case, the more challenging policy issues are related to our more narrow definition of private insurance. Certainly, objections to "two-tier" medicine in Canada appear to contemplate voluntary as opposed to government-mandated insurance schemes, although it is theoretically possible to have different "tiers" of public insurance.

In this section, we consider a number of issues related to mixed financing schemes: that is, schemes in which public and private insurance systems coexist in some ratio. As noted above, the potential for private insurance schemes to supplement the public scheme in a substantial way, or to fill "gaps" in coverage created by funding restrictions under the public plan, is a major concern of many advocates of a single payer system notwithstanding that there is already non-trivial private financing of specific health-care services in Canada. We do not compare all privately financed health care to the current Medicare system, since we do not believe that a fully privately-financed scheme is a relevant alternative. Not even the United States has an entirely privately-financed system.

Two-Tier Medicine

Perhaps the most frequently expressed concern about the coexistence of private and public sector insurance schemes is that two standards of health care will emerge with systematic inequities based upon income levels. Specifically, lower-income groups will be covered by a public insurance scheme that is severely circumscribed in what it covers and that is marked by poor quality, while higher-income groups will enjoy access to a much wider range of high quality treatments and procedures under their private coverage. These anticipated inequities cause concerns for critics even if higher-income individuals continue to make their full tax contributions to support Medicare. However, concerns about private insuring are magnified by perceptions that private insuring will ultimately erode public commitments to fund Medicare (Valpy, 1996).

1.   **Financing Commitments**   The basic notion here is straightforward. Non-price rationing is more likely to restrict higher-income individuals than lower-income individuals in purchasing health care. In principle, wealthier Canadians could offer to pay higher taxes to fund "improvements" to the public insurance scheme; however, the higher taxes paid will largely fund increased access to health care for other Canadians. That is, the wealthier cannot expect to receive anything close to a "dollar-for-dollar" improvement in the health care they receive under the public financing scheme as long as access to publicly-financed services is independent of the amount of taxes paid, while taxes are progressively related to income. Clearly, the correspondence between the amount spent on coverage and the level and quality of services received is much closer under private schemes. Hence, wealthier individuals can be expected to react to increased rationing under Medicare by purchasing private insurance.

Ignoring for the moment the possibility that the wealthier care about the level and quality of health care received by poorer citizens, this simple concern about two-tier medicine embodies several critical assumptions: (1) the demand for health care is a normal good; that is, it increases with real income; (2) consuming more health-care services is associated with better health, and (3) increased payments for private insurance will necessarily lead to reduced real resources being made available to the public insurance program.

The first assumption is innocuous. Studies are in agreement that the income elasticity of demand for health care is positive and, indeed, is probably greater than unity.[1] Hence, wealthier individuals are more likely to buy private insurance than poorer individuals. The second assumption is less innocuous. If purchasing greater access to health-care services does not result in improved health, equity concerns are mitigated, at least to the extent that such concerns are based upon differences in outcomes of health-care spending rather than upon differences in access, *per se*.[2] To be sure, the question that is potentially raised is why wealthier individuals would spend more on health care if such expenditures do not promise to translate into improved health status. One possible answer is that health-care expenditures are ultimately governed by the provider rather than by the patient, and that opportunistic exploitation of patients is more likely under privately-funded schemes than under publicly-funded ones.[3] Another less plausible answer is that individuals are buying "care-taking" as well as curing when buying health care. In any case, explicit rationing based upon cost-effectiveness or cost-utility makes it less likely that purchasing health care outside the Medicare system will accentuate health-outcome differences, since the less (clinically) effective treatments and procedures are more likely to be dropped from coverage under the publicly-financed scheme.

To our knowledge, there is no comprehensive theoretical or empirical treatment of the public finance dynamics of a mixed health-care financing system.[4] This is not surprising given the complex linkages between private and public health insurance financing efforts. Unfortunately, we are unable to provide a fully articulated and empirically-tested model of our own, although we do summarize some evidence from an unpublished companion piece of research. The following "stylized" discussion highlights the complex linkages discussed more fully in the companion piece. In our view, the complexity of the underlying issues serves as a caution against adopting the simplistic assumption that more private financing leads to less public financing.

For purposes of this discussion, it is assumed that there are two broad groups in Canadian society: those with above-average incomes and those with below-average incomes. The higher-income group pays a greater percentage of its earned income than the lower-income group to finance health care, but health care is financed out of general taxes rather than taxes specially earmarked for health care. Rationing, in this environment, can be seen as reducing the probabilities the two groups assign to receiving "timely" and/or comprehensive medical care. The probabilities will likely decline more for the higher-income group, since they have higher opportunity costs and, therefore, a lower tolerance for waiting in queues. If the benefits of preventing the relevant probabilities from declining exceed the costs of buying supplementary access to health care, say through private insurance, supplementary access will be purchased. The higher-income group is therefore more likely to purchase private insurance than is the lower-income group.

How might public funding of health care decline? With increased rationing, higher income individuals presumably see themselves as receiving less benefit from the Medicare system in an expected value sense. That is, they see themselves as being increasingly unlikely to be able to use the publicly-funded system in either as timely or as extensive a manner as before. If, as a group, they believed that they could reduce their tax obligations to fund the public system without further reducing their access to the public system, they will be inclined to lobby for lower taxes.[5] However, since they are above-average contributors to the system, such lobbying imposes a significant risk that their access to the publicly-financed system will be reduced even further, thereby obliging them to purchase even more private insurance. The result could be an adverse selection "spiral" of decreasing support for the public system. However, if private insurance is more expensive than public insurance for the same sets of services supplied, it might ultimately be more expensive for higher-income groups to replace the bulk (or all) of their public coverage by private coverage. In which case, it is unlikely that they will lobby strenuously for reduced funding of Medicare, particularly if they anticipate being able (satisfactorily) to obtain the bulk of their health-care services through the publicly-funded system. Equivalently, they are unlikely to lobby for reduced funding of Medicare if private insurance is required to pay for only part of the additional costs of health care, for example, "extra-billing" arrangements.

The incentive for the higher-income group to lobby for lower taxes is also mitigated by the fact that lobbying is costly. It can be particularly costly in this situation, since the lower-income group will be much larger than the higher-income group. Therefore, in a lobbying contest between the two groups, the cost per person will be much higher for the higher income group. It might be argued that the (smaller) higher income group will be more cohesive and therefore more effective than the lower-income group in lobbying, so that it will not have to spend as much in the aggregate to "outlobby" the lower income group. This proposition is questionable as the lower income group is likely to have lower health status than the upper income group resulting from less healthy lifestyle habits and, therefore, to have relatively high short-run financing needs. More pressing and more chronic financing needs may lead to the larger lower-income group being a more cohesive lobbying force than the higher-income group.

In short, the higher-income group will lobby for reduced taxes only if the expected tax savings exceed the expected costs of lobbying. Assuming that lobbying costs are subject to some indivisibilities, that is, relatively large minimum thresholds, it may well not pay the higher-income group to lobby for lower taxes, especially if lower taxes threaten to further reduce the access and scope of services they could expect to receive under the publicly-funded scheme. Obviously the more limited this access and scope becomes, the greater the incentive of the higher-income group to accept the risk of a further contraction of the publicly funded system, since the resulting tax savings are more likely to exceed the anticipated difference between the costs of supporting a full private insurance program and the costs of a full publicly funded program. This latter incentive follows from the fact that private coverage increasingly duplicates public coverage as the higher-income group supplements with more and more private insurance. Hence, there are increasingly fewer benefits foregone with the contraction of the Medicare scheme that have to be purchased with more expensive (per unit) private insurance. Put in other words, the relationship between private and public financing of health care may be discontinuous. Over some range of increased private financing, there may be little or no lobbying on the part of the higher-income group for reduced tax support of Medicare. But beyond some point, the incentive to lobby becomes substantial and might lead to a dynamically unstable situation in which successive lower tax contributions are made to Medicare by the higher-income group.

Opponents of the expansion of private financing implicitly must believe that the imposition of absolute prohibitions or, more realistically, the higher costs associated with accessing privately financed medicine, for example, forcing Canadians to visit clinics in the U.S. rather than in Canada, will "short-circuit" the potential dynamic linkage between increased private financing and reduced public financing. Assume, for the moment, that the Canadian government is successful in substantially raising the effective price to Canadians of obtaining private health insurance through a combination of policies. Would this increase or decrease the commitment of the higher income group to the Medicare system? Imagine that the higher income group is currently enjoying access to health care under Medicare that is considered "just adequate" to maintain a minimally acceptable state of health given existing opportunities to supplement publicly-supplied health care with selective private coverage. An increase in the effective price of privately-financed care would jeopardize maintenance of this minimally acceptable level of health. Previously being on the "razor's edge" in terms of their perceived value of public health care, the higher-income group may be tempted to abandon Medicare entirely. After all, if members of this group will suffer disability and possibly death, even though they are fully paying for Medicare, they have little incentive to save Medicare. Indeed, if they come to view the very existence of Medicare as a barrier to their attaining a minimally acceptable level of health, they have a strong incentive to lobby for its dismantling.

This example is highly stylized in its assumption that health status is binomial; that is, the individual is either minimally healthy or not. Most individuals are more or less healthy most of the time. However, the essential nature of the example is relevant. Many people at one or more discrete points in their lives will be on the margin between being functional or dysfunctional due to disease or injury, and will anticipate this possibility. If they anticipate a significant probability of being unable to access the Medicare system, their commitment to that system may well erode, even though the probability refers to individual events rather than to continuous "states-of-nature". Take, as an example, the treatment of cardiac disease. Many individuals can anticipate cardiac disease at some point in their lives. Rationing that significantly reduces perceived future access of the higher-income group to treatments for cardiac disease could significantly erode their support for Medicare well before the onset of disease.

The implication of the preceding analysis is that impeding access to privately-financed treatments of relatively mundane ailments and complaints may be less likely to trigger a defection of support for Medicare than will impeding access to treatments of episodic, but potentially catastrophic, events. If this assumption is accurate, it has certain implications for policy makers seeking to maintain tax funding support levels for Medicare: that is, avoid imposing increased rationing for procedures that are highly significant (albeit episodic) to preserving a minimally healthy state of being. It is not obvious whether resources would be saved by increased rationing of more mundane procedures. Moreover, given the potential for the very wealthy to buy significant treatments and procedures anywhere in the world, efforts to restrict domestic private funding initiatives are more likely to harm middle-income individuals. Thus, concerns about the intrinsic unfairness of some individuals being able to afford private insurance and others not will still exist even if the government makes it necessary for Canadians to buy privately-financed medical care outside the country.

2. **Real Resource Transfers and Efficiency Implications**   A more subtle critique of permitting private health insurance maintains that even if tax revenues available to the public sector are constant, the cost of medical inputs to the government financial insurance scheme will be bid up by the increased demand from the private insurance sector. As a result,

the same level of public sector expenditure would buy fewer health-care services than previously. The more inelastic the supply of health-care inputs, the more relevant is this concern.[6] Assuming for the moment that the long-run supply of health-care inputs is relatively inelastic, another implicit assumption underlying this critique is that there will be no overall efficiency gains from introducing private insurance. That is, the introduction of private insurance will simply bid-up factor prices in the health-care sector, thereby leading to lower quantity (or quality) of health care provided under the public insurance scheme.

In opposition to this critique is the possibility that the competition provided by private insurance plans might stimulate efficiency improvements and/or quality changes in the public plan. For example, such competition might stimulate an increased range and variety of insurance offerings that better reflect differences in the preferences of consumers. It might also encourage new and better ways to monitor expenditures made by health-care providers, as well as more careful and effective evaluations of the health outcomes of different medical procedures.[7]

There is a very extensive literature on the relationship between market structure and the introduction and diffusion of new technology.[8] Simplifying somewhat, the results are broadly consistent with a conclusion that increased competition encourages a faster rate of introduction and utilization of new production and administrative procedures. The few available studies of the health insurance sector tend to support this conclusion. For example, Goldberg and Greenberg (1995) describe the responses of the Blue Cross/Blue Shield insurer in Rhode Island to the entry of a new competitor. Among other things, Blue Cross/Blue Shield became a more "prudent" buyer of medical services: in particular, it negotiated lower payments to physicians with no noticeable reduction in the quantity or quality of coverage provided. It also introduced a new product with a more comprehensive benefit package than its traditional plan. Some studies of the reaction of Blue Cross/Blue Shield insurers to competition are consistent with the Rhode Island experience. Some of these studies will be reviewed in a later section.

Glennerster and Matsaganis (1993) review the early experience with health-care reforms in the United Kingdom. In particular, they evaluate the impact of making District Health Authorities the purchasers of hospital and community health services, on the one hand, and giving family doctors the money to buy these services on behalf of their patients, on the other hand. While the District Health Authorities and the family doctors were not competing in the strict sense of the word, the practical effect of the reform was to encourage a diversity of "buying" plans.[9] The authors conclude that comparing areas with many general practitioner fundholders to those with fewer, there is little doubt that the substantial presence of fundholders enhances the competitive environment. Most of the practices secured some 'improvements" in the services they received from hospitals, for example in laboratory testing arrangements. Changes were also made in the ways that services were delivered to patients. The latter included opening facilities for minor operations and transferring a large part of outpatient work to the physicians' own premises. These changes were seen as improving the convenience and utility of the services delivered to patients. On the other hand, District Health Authorities were relatively cautious about demanding changes on the part of providers. The authors ascribe the difference in behaviour to the bureaucratic and political inertia in the public District Health Authorities.

To be sure, the evidence cited above attesting to certain benefits from competition among health insurance plans can (and has) been criticized on a variety of grounds. Perhaps the broadest criticism is that the changes encouraged by competition identified in the relevant studies may not be welfare-improving, on balance, and/or that they have associated costs which exceed any benefits. One particular criticism is that administrative costs increase disproportionately to the increase in the number of independent insurers given economies of scale in administrative activities (Deber, Mhatie, and Baker, 1994). A number of studies provide strong empirical support for the proposition that there are substantial economies of scale in the administration of health insurance plans (Evans *et. al.*, 1989). However, the relevant issue is whether the benefits generated by a diversity of plans more than offsets any additional "deadweight" costs of administration. Glennerster and Matsaganis (1993) argue that the increase in administration costs associated with the fundholders' purchasing experience in the United Kingdom was modest. Moreover, they argue that if consumers are willing to pay any additional costs of administration, they are presumably revealing through their preferences that they see the associated benefits as outweighing any additional costs.[10]

Most health-care economists have been loath to accept revealed consumer preference as an indicator of whether competition improves economic welfare. The primary objection is that consumers are typically imperfectly informed about the benefits associated with health-care services generally and with the expected benefits of different health insurance plans specifically. As a consequence, market-based "survivor" tests of alternative health-care plans are not necessarily reliable indicators of associated welfare changes. This caveat is particularly relevant to the extent that public sector plans explicitly or implicitly subsidize private plans. For example, concerns have been expressed (backed by evidence) that private plans will "cream-skim" by refusing to enroll high-risk individuals or individuals with identifiable pre-conditions which make them potentially high cost insurees or by charging appropriately higher premiums to such individuals.[11] If the public plans do not engage in such selective rating practices, they will have higher costs than private plans and will, consequently, be at a competitive disadvantage in competing with private insurers on the basis of premiums charged, absent subsidies from tax revenues. Equivalently, public sector plans may cover complicated and expensive procedures that private sector plans refuse to cover, and the "rates" charged by the public sector plans, that is, the taxes required to fund the public plans, would have to reflect the higher average costs of the publicly insured services. Presumably, healthier individuals would not want to pay these higher rates, thereby exacerbating the "adverse selection" problem facing the public sector plan.[12]

The impact of introducing private insurance on real costs associated with providing health care is also complicated by the existence of "dead-weight" costs associated with government tax and transfer programs. These costs encompass distortions in behaviour that reduce economic growth by reducing incentives to work and save on the margin. Many have argued that public financing plays a collective purchasing role and that, as a monopsonist, the state is able to monitor the mix of services, as well as their overall level, more efficiently than a collection of private insurers. The point to bear in mind is that such pecuniary cost savings do not necessarily reduce economy-wide costs which include dead-weight costs. Moreover, set against the potential for the public insurer to act as a monopsonist is the consideration that public insurers arguably have less incentive to be efficient than private insurers (McGuire, Fenn, and Mayhew, 1994).

In short, theoretical considerations do not necessarily support a conclusion that increasing the ratio of private to total health-care financing will necessarily lead to higher overall costs of producing any given level of health care. Moreover, the available evidence does not support a conclusion that changing the ratio of private to public funding of health care affects relative expenditures on health care. For example, Besley and Gouveia (1994) find for a sample of OECD countries that the correlation between changes in the government share of health-care expenditures and changes in the share of health-care expenditures in GDP is positive but statistically insignificant at usual confidence levels. Moreover, there is no significant correlation between changes in the government share of health-care expenditures and the growth rate of the relative price level for health care.

Subsidy

To the extent that physicians and other providers bill both public and private insurers ("extra billing"), a concern exists that the public insurance scheme will subsidize the private scheme. Specifically, the concern is that physicians and other suppliers of health-care services will use resources acquired under the public insurance plan to provide services for which compensation is paid under private sector plans. This is certainly one of the major objections raised by critics of private clinics operating in Alberta, who argue that not all of the incremental costs of treating patients in the private clinics are incorporated in the extra-billings charged by the physicians (In June, 1996, the Government of Alberta announced that it would outlaw extra-billing by physicians). Taxpayers are therefore allegedly subsidizing the activities of private clinics which, if true, would make further suspect any welfare evaluation of clinics based upon the revealed preferences of customers.[13]

It is extremely difficult to evaluate claims of subsidy in the case of jointly-supplied services such as those provided by physicians who use both hospital facilities and private clinics to treat patients. Patients (or their employers) would have paid Medicare premiums, and to insist that clinic operators not bill at all under the public insurance program would, in effect, amount to subsidizing the public insurance program by taxing individuals who do not use public facilities. In principle, the "solution" to this potential problem has been extensively discussed in the literature dealing with competition in public utilities. There has been a long-standing concern, for example, in the telecommunications industry that local service suppliers will use their ownership of the local network to subsidize their competitive long-distance affiliates. Local service suppliers might "undercharge" their long-distance affiliates for local access, while "overcharging" other users of local access services.[14] A suggested remedy is to require integrated carriers to charge an imputed price for services supplied to their integrated affiliates which is calculated using efficient pricing rules. These rules would reflect all explicit costs as well as all implicit costs associated with supplying the relevant services. Adoption of an explicit efficient pricing rule that is uniformly applied to all services supplied by hospitals, whether those services are supplied to physicians paid by the public scheme or private scheme, mitigates the potential for opportunistic behaviour by physicians who bill patients under either scheme.[15]

In principle, medical service inputs could be priced for purposes of use by physicians and other professionals under either public or private sector health-care plans. If the primary issue is to avoid subsidizing private medicine, the precision of the price-setting rule is less important than the uniform application of the rule regardless of the nature of the payment plan under which physicians are reimbursed for their services. To be sure, the notion of pricing access to health-care facilities and equipment (even nationally) may strike many as being akin to implementing user charges. Moreover, the concern might again be raised that private insurance plans that serve clients with above-average incomes will be able to bid public sector facilities away from physicians operating under the public system if hospitals charge efficient (that is, incremental cost-based) prices. Efficient pricing might therefore contribute to less equality of access to health-care services. However valid this concern, it does not gainsay the point that a potential problem of subsidization is not an intractable obstacle to the implementation of private insurance schemes in competition with public schemes.

In fact, the main concern surrounding extra-billing is that it effectively makes it less costly for wealthier Canadians to buy better quality medical care, since they are required only to pay the incremental costs for medical services outside the public scheme. Such incremental costs may be associated with, for example, faster service or the use of newer technology. Unlike complete private financing, partial private financing, such as an extra-billing regime, does not leave more financial resources available to fund the public system. To this extent, extra-billing is likely to be more controversial than a regime where the wealthier can only utilize separate, complete private financing.

Summary of Main Theoretical Arguments

Credible potential objections to allowing the growth of privately-financed insurance programs in Canada rest upon three major arguments: (1) that the willingness of individuals to pay for Medicare through direct and indirect taxes will be eroded by an ability to buy private insurance; (2) that the growth of private insurance will inevitably lead to two-tier medicine with those able to buy private insurance enjoying higher quality medicine and/or access to a wider range of treatments or to more timely access to treatments; (3) that competition between insurance plans will lead to higher costs, through the sacrifice of administrative economies of scale, as well as inefficient cross-subsidization of private care and the loss of monopsony purchasing advantages associated with a single government payer.

Any theoretical consideration of the willingness-to-pay objection should acknowledge several realities. First, wealthy Canadians can currently buy health care in a world market, and the addition of private financing alternatives in Canada may add relatively little to their current set of opportunities. Second, the notion that there is a potential "dollar-for-dollar" tradeoff between the willingness to fund the public system and expenditures in the private system is highly unrealistic. Individuals purchasing private insurance are unlikely to find it worthwhile to lobby for reductions in their taxes, on the margin, especially if they derive satisfaction from knowing that other individuals are continuing to benefit from the publicly funded system. At some point, increased private funding may lead to substantial lobbying efforts to truncate or abandon the financing commitment to the public scheme. However, this is unlikely to occur until a substantial number of Canadians have turned to private insurance for a significant portion of their health-care needs.[16]

Indeed, it seems more likely to us that support for, or at least tolerance of, the publicly-funded system will be eroded more quickly by perceptions that there are non-trivial probabilities of being unable to maintain "adequate levels" of health because of rationing in the public system combined with restricted access to private sector alternatives. Put slightly differently, if a substantial number of higher-income individuals perceive a decrease in ready access to publicly-funded treatments that they see as actually or potentially important to maintaining an acceptable expected "status of health", and if this is combined with a perception that the government is restricting their access to privately-financed alternatives to prevent "two-tier" medicine, they are more likely to incur the costs associated with lobbying down the current Medicare system. In short, efforts by government to deny individuals access to supplemental private insurance may encourage those individuals to view their financing choice as being dichotomous; that is, lobby to terminate the existing publicly financed regime or accept significant risks of being effectively underinsured and undersupplied with respect to health-care services.

Empirical evidence discussed in the next section casts strong doubt on the relevance of "slippery slope" arguments against allowing private financing of health care. Specifically, there is no evidence that the existence of private insurance alternatives leads to the suppression or extinction of publicly financed alternatives. In fact, major publicly-funded systems have emerged, and grown, in many jurisdictions where private insurance was the dominant delivery approach. Moreover, in jurisdictions where private insurance has increased in importance, including Canada, there is no evidence of a substantial erosion of public support for the publicly-funded programs.

Both theory and evidence support a concern that access to health care is less "democratic" under privately-funded schemes. However, this is not the same thing as saying that allowing increased private health-care financing will create gross inequities in either access to health or health status. It certainly does not imply that poorer individuals will be worse off than they would be absent any private insurance alternatives. To the extent that wealthier individuals are more likely to "drop off" waiting lists than poorer individuals, the latter may enjoy improved access to publicly-financed health care, at least in terms of faster access. A concern sometimes expressed here is that wealthier individuals will be able to bid away more qualified physicians and other inputs, leaving the publicly-financed scheme to operate with lower quality inputs. Clearly this is not a necessary result to the extent that "high quality" physicians and so forth are available in relatively elastic supply. Given the perpetual excess supply of candidates for medical school as well as a virtually unlimited supply of potential immigrant medical personnel, it is implausible to suggest that the quality of the publicly-financed system will be jeopardized in the long run by a shortage of skilled labour or capital.[17] Moreover, there need be little upward long-run pressure on prices of inputs ultimately paid for by the public insurance scheme, barring deliberate policies by government to restrict the growth in supply of inputs.[18]

Empirical evidence supports the position that physicians do not abandon the publicly financed program for private schemes under mixed financing regimes. Where mixed financing schemes exist, many physicians work for both systems. Indeed, greater security and ease of payment under the public system usually means that physicians will work for lower fees under the publicly-financed system. A growing concern among critics of a mixed financing regime is that physicians will use publicly-funded facilities to supply services paid for privately. Where services are truly jointly-supplied, the potential problem of cross-subsidization is real. However, it is not clear that there is a joint supply problem at work in the case-at-hand. Indeed, it would seem relatively easy to identify which procedures were being supplied to publicly-financed patients versus privately-financed patients. If public capital was being used as a complementary input to the supply of services to privately-insured patients, it would be possible to establish and charge an appropriate "rental" price. In fact, it seems more appropriate to consider the cross-subsidy concern as an objection to doctors "hedging" their exposure to competitive medical markets by using the public scheme as a steady source of income. This interpretation seems consistent with government objections to extra-billing under the Medicare system. However, unless motivated by envy, this objection is illogical, since allowing such hedging enables the public scheme to purchase physician services more cheaply than otherwise would be possible.

None of the foregoing analysis is mean to gainsay the basic argument that a *significant* reduction in public sector funding of health care would lead to reduced access on the part of lower-income groups, a result deemed by most, if not all Canadians, to be undesirable. The point here is that any such reduction would be the outcome of a policy decision to reduce government expenditures and not the necessary result of wealthier Canadians buying some of their health care through private markets for insurance.

CHAPTER SIX

Evidence on the Performance of "Mixed" Systems

In this section, we review some evidence on the consequences of allowing competition among health insurers. It should be noted at the outset that a substantial amount of the relevant evidence bears upon competition among either private sector insurers or public sector insurers, but not necessarily between public and private insurers. Nevertheless, the experience with competition among private insurers sheds light upon major concerns raised about a mixed financing regime.

The evidence covers the following experiences: first, we examine the extensive experience of the United Kingdom with its mixed financing regime in the inter-war period. Second, we look at the experience of the United States with Medicare and Medicaid, as well as with competition experienced by Blue Cross and Blue Shield from a range of insurers including those affiliated with health maintenance organizations (HMOs) and preferred provider organizations (PPOs). It can be argued that Blue Cross and Blue Shield for many years were quasi-public insurers, inasmuch as they were non-profit organizations that received discounts from hospitals not received by commercial insurers. In exchange, Blue Cross and Blue Shield agreed to be essentially universal providers. Third, we review the experience of Canada prior to the full implementation of the universal Medicare plan. In particular, the experience of Canada under a largely private insurance system offers some insight into the potential consequences of moving away from a single-payer system in Canada. Moreover, the different speed with which provinces moved to implement public insurance plans offers some basis of comparison across mixed insurance regimes. Finally, we examine contemporary international experience with mixed financing regimes.

Background

As noted earlier, while the bulk of health-care funding in virtually all developed countries is public (or highly regulated by government), there is a non-trivial amount of private financing. This applies even in a country with a single government payer, such as Canada. For example, while the *Canada Health Act* of 1984 guarantees health services to all citizens, it excludes most adult dental services, optometry, physiotherapy, osteopathy, ambulance services, dietetics, hearing aids, psychology, pharmaceuticals, and other ancillary services, except when provided in hospitals (Blank, 1994:108). Such services are paid for out-of-pocket and/or by privately-sponsored insurance plans. More recently, Canada's first dial-a-doctor service was established. It is being monitored by the federal Ministry of Health. The service, which costs $3.99 a minute and is not covered by Medicare, is taking calls from all over the country. It was launched by 10 Fredericton physicians using 1-900 technology. The service is believed to be the first in North America offering people live advice from doctors for a fee (*The Globe and Mail*, December 1, 1995:A6).

As another example, New Zealand funds hospital care through general taxation but, except with regard to particular categories of patients, depends on direct user payment for most primary care. In Belgium, the self-employed and employers are covered only for the heavy risks of inpatient care and for certain diseases such as cancer and tuberculosis. Immigrants, the wealthy and the very poor are not covered. Where coverage is not universal, voluntary health insurance fills most of the gaps left by statutory insurance. At the same time, the disabled, the poor and so forth are often exempt from paying for the health-care services they receive. In Ireland, only low income individuals are covered for primary care. Those not covered have to pay privately for care outside hospitals (Abel-Smith and Mossiados, 1994). In the Netherlands, private health insurance companies often cover normal medical expenses not covered by the Exceptional Medical Expenses Act. While the private insurance schemes vary in nature and coverage, costs for medicine and general practice are not always included under the coverage. Sometimes such costs are insured only over a certain maximum or with a co-payment (HSU 2000, 1994).[1]

Private financing of health-care expenditures also exists for supplementation or "topping-up" the quantity of health care consumed under public financed programs. The best example of this is the French system, where there is a second tier of providers with above-average reputations or "market value" which are allowed to charge patients fees above the levels regulated by national convention. The patients are reimbursed by government but only up to the "nomenclature" levels and so are responsible for the difference. These differences can be either reimbursed by supplementary private health insurance or paid out-of-pocket. Similar schemes apply to other European countries, and supplementation is also common in the limited public provision existing in the United States. Specifically, the Medicare programme which covers the elderly and disabled can be supplemented by an array of so-called Medigap private insurance plans.[2]

The point here is not necessarily that some minimal amount of private financing of health care is necessarily a good thing. Rather, it is that the United States is not the only example of a health-care financing system in which private interests play a role. As such, rational debate about the appropriate role for private financing in Canada tends to become stifled if the United States is held up as the only counter-factual to a truly universal, publicly-financed system. Moreover, it is important to remember that some Canadians will have access to private health care regardless of Canadian government policy, to the extent that they can afford to purchase medical services in the United States. Indeed, a recent survey indicates that about one percent of British Columbians with heart disease currently have heart surgery performed outside of Canada in preference to waiting for surgery in British Columbia. For Canada as a whole, approximately 0.5 percent of patients have their heart surgery performed outside the country (Ramsay and Walker, 1995). Moreover, anecdotal evidence suggests that the U.S. medical system is seen by an increasing number of Canadians as a supplementary source of supply to the Canadian system. One indication is an increase in advertising in Canada by U.S. suppliers of health-care services. Another is the emergence of Canadian companies that market private insurance for non-emergency treatment outside of Canada and that facilitate receipt of diagnostic testing in the United States (Ramsay and Walker, 1995).

Ontario Blue Cross has apparently begun advertising coverage gaps in the Ontario Health Insurance Plan (OHIP). Among the services not covered by OHIP but covered by Blue Cross are prescription drugs, eyeglasses and contact lenses, dental care, semi-private hospital rooms, private physiotherapy, ambulance service, and out-of-country medical treatment (other than hospital coverage). The Ontario Health Minister said she saw no need for concern about the Blue Cross initiative since "services are certainly not being privatized in the important components which keep people healthy" (Mickleburg, 1994:A4).

It might also be pointed out that while there has been a broad convergence among countries in the public sector share of total health-care expenditures, substantial differences still existed in the early 1960s. These differences are illustrated by data in Table 6.1. The data support an inference that significant private funding of health care in many countries did not prevent the absolute and relative growth of publicly-funded schemes. They also underscore the relevance of looking to examples other than the United States for evidence about the consequences of mixed financing regimes.

Inter-War (and Earlier) Periods in the United Kingdom

During the period between the First and Second World Wars, there was a substantial amount of private financing of health-care expenditures

Table 6.1

Public Share of Total Health Expenditures: Selected Countries for 1960	
Country	Percentage
UK	85
Italy	83
Sweden	72
Belgium	62
Japan	60
Spain	58
France	58
Canada	42
U.S.	25

Source: Besley and Gouveia (1994:208).

in the United Kingdom. Specifically, publicly-funded hospital services accounted for around 30 percent of total spending on health care, the voluntary hospitals accounted for approximately 12 percent, around 10 percent of the total spending went on the National Health Insurance scheme and most of the remainder — around 40 to 50 percent — could be attributed to personal expenditure on doctors' and dentists' fees and on self-medication.[3]

The inter-war experience of the United Kingdom provides some indirect insight into the issue of whether and how the financing of public health insurance is affected by the size and scope of private insurance. The experience suggests that a relatively large private funding commitment did not prevent the growth of public funding. In relation to GNP, public expenditure on health care expanded steadily from 0.8 percent in 1920 to 1.6 percent by 1930, reaching 1.9 percent by 1932 and retaining a 1.9 percent share by 1938. By contrast, in relation to GNP, private health-care expenditures rose from 0.93 percent in 1920 to a peak of almost 1.5 percent by 1932 and thereafter remained fairly level. Hence, the proportion of GNP devoted to health services approximately doubled in less than 20 years. The shares of private and public expenditure in the total were relatively even, but with a drift towards the public sector over time.

It can be argued that the relationship between private and public financing of health care is more complex than the relationship suggested by simply comparing shares of financing in GDP as in the preceding paragraph. Indeed, Gray (1994) suggests that the growth of public financing may have restricted the growth of the privately-financed sector. For example, the ability of voluntary hospitals to meet rising demand was curtailed in part because their main source of income, charitable gifts and donations, was reduced by surtaxes and death duties. Ironically, the latter were introduced, in part, to pay for increased public health care. While an analysis that held all other influences explicitly constant would obviously support more confident conclusions, a simple interpretation of the evidence does not support arguments that the existence of a significant level of private health insurance inevitably precipitates a significant contraction of public health-care expenditures. Indeed, during the inter-war period in the United Kingdom, public spending on health services grew more rapidly than on most other items of public expenditure.

The impacts of funding mix on the efficiency of service provision and the distribution of benefits and costs are more difficult to summarize. There is evidence suggesting that incompatibilities between the funding regimes led to certain inefficiencies. For example, while hospital services were not covered by the National Health Insurance (NHI) scheme, the incentive structure operating within the NHI's capitation system encouraged doctors to pass patients quickly on to hospital rather than to less expensive out-patient departments.

The growth of publicly-financed health care arguably increased access to health-care services among lower-income families. This can be inferred from the following data. In absolute amounts, expenditure per person on medical services amongst middle-class families was roughly three to four times that of working-class families. Fees to health professionals were the largest single item of health-care expenditure among both working-class and middle-class families. The NHI covered fees to health professionals, but middle-class wage earners were generally above the earnings limit for NHI membership. The public funding of hospital services was arguably less redistributive towards lower-income families. This is because funding for public hospitals was generated from the local tax base, and the ability of local authorities to generate revenue was more limited in depressed areas than in prosperous parts of the country. Nevertheless, the types of hospital care provided by the voluntary and public sectors differed greatly. Voluntary hospitals had no legal obligation to accept all classes of patients and had long discriminated against chronic and other uneconomic cases. For example, the provision of in-patient care for infectious, tubercular and chronic patients was left largely to the public sector.

The evidence also suggests that the quality of public hospitals was, if anything, higher than that of private hospitals. In particular, the transfer of ownership of many hospitals from Poor Law to local authorities was followed in many instances by improvements to quality of care. Consultant staff were hired in increasing numbers on a part-time basis from the voluntary hospitals. The rate and expansion of nursing staff exceeded that in the voluntary hospitals, and recruitment of nurses was assisted by hours of work and rates of pay that were better than those prevailing in voluntary hospitals. Indeed, the voluntary hospitals' failure to evolve a self-regulatory apparatus resulted in a continuing failure to meet either the demands of the market or even some clinical consensus on medical need. Financial exigencies resulted in the voluntary sector neglecting vital expenditures and requiring public funding to avoid bankruptcy.

Digby and Bosanquet (1988) discuss even earlier British experience with state health insurance. Specifically, they discuss the (panel system) public health insurance scheme that was introduced in Britain by the *National Insurance Act* of 1911 and came into effect in 1913.[4] Initially, the Act included those aged between 16 and 70 and employed in manual labour or in non-manual jobs with an income less than £160 per year. The system was gradually increased to cover a greater proportion of the working population. In Great Britain, 13.7 million people were insured by 1914 and 19.2 million by 1936, an increase from 47 percent to 54 percent of the adult population. For these panel patients, medical practitioners were paid a capitation fee by the government.

It should be noted that the panel system scheme was introduced at a time when many Britons had similar private prepayment schemes. About half the working population in 1905 was covered by contracts between friendly societies or industrial works and physicians, whereby the physician would provide specified medical treatment in return for a small fee. There were also medical clubs and subscriptions clubs operated by physicians. The panel system was not a comprehensive medical insurance scheme. For example, it did not cover hospital expenditures; however, it was no less comprehensive than many other private pre-payment schemes.

Most interwar physicians in Britain adopted a "mixed" cash and panel practice. One observation was that panel doctors with large public insurance patient loads tried to economize on their time as much as possible in order to attend their more remunerative private practices; however, this preference reflects the difference between the public scheme's capitation payment and the fee-for-service practice of private insurance approaches. The panel system clearly provided incentives for working-class patients to consult doctors much more frequently than before; however, there was also greater use of doctors made by non-insured patients owing largely to improvements in medical practice. Nevertheless, public insurance did contribute to lower-income groups consuming more medical care. Household expenditure surveys in 1938-39 showed that working-class households allocated less than three percent of their total expenditures to medical care purchased outside the public insurance program. Women and children in particular, who were not covered under the panel system, relied heavily upon free services offered by out-patient clinics in hospitals and maternity and infant welfare clinics. Among the poorest families, doctors were sent for to treat uninsured dependents only for serious illnesses. Conversely, it was estimated by the British Medical Association in 1926 that doctors made marginally more visits to private patients than to those covered under the panel system (3.96 visits per year compared to 3.77 visits).

Some evidence bearing upon concerns that patients covered by private insurance will receive "better" medical care than those covered by public insurance is also provided by the panel system experience. One concern expressed was that doctors spent less time with publicly-insured patients than with their private patients. Again, this is attributable to the capitation payment system that was largely in use under the panel system. Where alternative fee-for-service payment schemes operated under the public insurance program, practitioners were more attentive to their patients and, in contrast to areas where the capitation scheme operated, there were no complaints by insured patients against their doctors. Overall, much of the difference in patient care was associated with patient convenience. Private patients could more easily obtain a visit in their own homes from their doctors. When coming to the doctor's surgery, it was common for private patients to have an appointment and to enter through the front door, where panel patients entered through the surgery door and had to wait their turn to see the doctor. Rural practice was not as sophisticated as urban practice so that the differences between the two categories of patient were apparently smaller.

In summary, the British inter-war experience supports some generalizations about health-care financing but not others. In particular, it supports the basic notion that access to health care among lower-income individuals and individuals with pre-existing health conditions will be expanded by the growth of public funding. It does not support an assertion that the growth of public funding is constrained or reversed by the existence of significant levels of private funding. It also fails to support the notion that publicly-funded care is inevitably of significantly "lower-quality" than privately funded care. While there is some evidence that the National Health Service was able to use monopsony power in bargaining with professional groups, especially doctors, in the early years, there is no consistent evidence that overall efficiency in the delivery of health-care services was affected by the growth of publicly-financed health care. Moreover, the ability to exercise monopsony power in bargaining has been significantly eroded over time by a reduced growth rate in the supply of physicians relative to the growth in demand.

The U.S. Experience

The U.S. experience with health insurance offers several perspectives on the policy issues raised by a mixed funding regime. For example, the emergence of public funding under Medicare and Medicaid offers additional evidence of the emergence of publicly funded programs under a (hitherto) purely privately-funded regime. The coexistence of two large publicly-funded programs alongside a plethora of privately-funded plans also offers a perspective on concerns about two-tier medicine under a mixed financing regime. Another feature of the U.S. experience is the reaction of Blue Cross/Blue Shield insurance plans to competition from other private insurance plans, especially from Health Maintenance Organizations (HMOs). As noted in an earlier section, Blue Cross/Blue Shield plans can be seen as quasi-public insurance programs. Specifically, they are non-profit organizations which receive favourable tax and related treatments from the government. In return, they are expected to forebear from excluding patients on the basis of pre-conditions and the like.[5]

1. **The Blue Cross/Blue Shield Experience**   In the late 1970s, there were 74 regional Blue Cross plans throughout the United States with more than 38 percent of the nation's population enrolled. They faced competition from an established group of commercial insurers, as well as an emerging group of HMO organizations. In one study, Goldberg and Greenberg (1980) examined the impact that private insurers, especially HMOs, had on Blue Cross Association plans in terms of hospital utilization as a proxy for cost efficiency and the "richness" of the benefits package offered as a proxy for responsiveness to consumers. They found that HMOs have a pro-competitive effect on Blue Cross plans by inducing them to reduce hospital utilization in those areas where the HMO has the largest market share. This was an expected result, since HMOs primarily compete for customers on the basis of lower prices and therefore should be especially cost-conscious. Conversely, there was no relationship between Blue Cross hospital utilization rates and the market shares of commercial insurers. This too was an expected result, as commercial insurers do not focus on cost reduction but (rather) on the promotion of services.[6] There was also weaker statistical evidence that competition from HMOs stimulates Blue Cross plans to increase their benefit package.

In a subsequent analysis of HMO growth, Goldberg and Greenberg (1981) examine variations in state HMO market share in 1976 and market share growth between 1966 and 1976. In contrast to their previous findings, they report that hospital costs are positively associated with HMO's 1976 market share, as well as with HMO growth. They explain this result on the basis that an environment of increasing hospital costs encourages both the establishment of new HMOs and the growth of all HMOs. However, it is difficult to explain how a larger HMO market share can contribute to lower hospital utilization rates while at the same time being associated with higher hospital costs, unless a reduction in hospital utilization leads to more severe cases, on average, being treated.

Hay and Leahy (1984) attempt to correct the statistical shortcomings that they argue plague the earlier Goldberg and Greenberg studies. They use a much larger cross-sectional sample to evaluate the impacts of competition among health-care plans for the U.S. in 1978. They also standardize for several factors that may bias Goldberg and Greenberg's earlier results. The market for health plans in that year consisted of four distinct segments: (1) government plans (primarily Medicare and Medicaid) accounting for 20.9 percent of insured persons; (2) Blue Cross/Blue Shield accounting for 37.5 percent of insured persons; (3) commercial insurers accounting for 40.5 percent; and (4) alternative delivery systems (primarily HMOs) accounting for 3.1 percent. Hay and Leahy conclude that competition among health-care plans tends to reduce health-care expenditures and utilization rates.[7]

It should be noted that the Hay and Leahy finding does not necessarily imply that unrestricted private sector competition in the financing of health care will lead to lower overall costs of supplying health-care insurance. As noted earlier, administrative costs increase disproportionately to the number of financiers. As well, private financing schemes may require more regulatory supervision than public schemes. Nevertheless, their finding does point to the potential for some amount of competition to encourage economization on the part of service providers, contrary to the view that a universal government health-care plan can reduce costs by essentially buying the services of suppliers as a monopsonist.

2. **Government Insurance Schemes** The two main public insurance programs in the United States are Medicare, which covers senior citizens, and Medicaid which covers low-income Americans. Recent evidence supports the inference drawn from virtually all other studies that coverage offered by public insurance plans increases utilization of health-care services by low-income groups. However, the experience under Medicaid is somewhat complex. For example, Currie and Thomas (1995) compare the medical care received by children covered by Medicaid, by private

health insurance and those with no insurance coverage at all. They find that there are substantial differences in the impact of public and private health insurance and that these effects also differ between blacks and whites. White children on Medicaid tend to have more doctor checkups than any other children, and white children on Medicaid or a private insurance plan have a higher number of doctor visits for illness. In contrast, for black children, neither Medicaid nor private insurance coverage is associated with any advantage in terms of the number of doctor visits for illness. Furthermore, black children with private coverage are no more likely than those with no coverage to have doctor checkups. On the other hand, black Medicaid children are more likely than either group to have checkups.

Other studies also suggest that government sponsored health-care programs *per se* do not result in identical rates of utilization across different groups in society. For example, Hayward *et. al.* (1988) found in a large sample of Americans that being uninsured predicted lower access to medical care. This was an expected result. Less expected was their finding that poverty was also an independent predictor of lower access to care. Holding income constant, blacks were more likely than whites to have unmet medical needs. Even among the poor and racial and ethnic minorities who can obtain insurance, there continue to be problems of access, although the source of these problems is unclear. An implication of this and related studies is that concerns about "two-tiers" of access emerging under a mixed financing system overlook the fact that differential access exists under the purely publicly-financed system — a point already noted in our earlier discussion of waiting lists in Canada.[8]

U.S. Medicaid is a federal-state matching program that is driven by eligibility policies which vary across states. Moreover there is wide variation in covered benefits among the states. Hence, it is somewhat difficult to compare coverage provided by Medicaid to coverage provided by private insurance schemes. Some states place no limits on reimbursable services, while others cap the number of hospital days and physician visits. Many states reimburse providers under Medicaid rates so far below customary charges that many physicians refuse to see Medicaid patients (Aaron, 1991:63). On the other hand, Medicaid appears more generous than most private insurance in payments for pharmaceuticals, ambulatory care, long-term care and support services (Fox, 1992). While states are in the process of trying to reduce coverage benefits under Medicaid, it is not clear that these efforts are any more aggressive than efforts being made by private insurers to restrict benefit claims made by their clients, or by employers offering managed care benefits to their employees.

The Canadian Experience

Medicare developed incrementally from two voluntary cost-shared programs — the *Hospital Insurance and Diagnostic Services Act* (1957) and the *Medical Care Act* (1966-67). The federal government provided funds to provincial plans as long as those plans complied with specified terms and conditions.[9] Federal support for provincially-run social welfare programs, many of them health related, was consolidated in another cost-shared program, the Canada Assistance Plan of 1966. The latter program was means-tested, unlike Medicare. It was used by the provinces to subsidize a range of health-related services and benefits, such as homemaker services, case-work, counseling and services for the disabled. Over time, revisions have taken place to funding arrangements primarily resulting in decreased growth in federal transfers, reductions in the proportion of those transfers paid in cash (rather than tax transfers) and placement of greater responsibility for spending and its control on the provinces. The *Canada Health Act* of 1984, among other things, established financial penalties for provinces allowing direct charges to patients for insured services including extra-billing by physicians and hospital user charges.

Patterns for Canada reinforce what is true for every other developed country we have considered. Namely, the existence of a predominantly privately funded health-care system did not prevent the emergence of an essentially all publicly-funded program. To be sure, the emergence and growth of the Medicare system was neither quick, nor without rancorous debate between different groups. However, it was acknowledged from the outset that a universal comprehensive plan would probably drive private insurance companies from the market (Swartz, 1993). Hence, one could expect substantial private sector resistance to the implementation of a comprehensive universal government plan. Moreover, governments had reservations based upon concerns about what such a program would cost and whether it could be funded.

Perhaps of even greater significance with respect to possible interactions between public and private financing, increases in private expenditures on health care have taken place in Canada in recent years, in part as a reaction to cost containment strategies in the public sector (Thall, 1994). The absolute increases in private expenditures on health care have not been associated with decreases in public expenditures as suggested by the data in Table 1.4. Especially noteworthy is the increase in private financing of pharmaceuticals. Clearly, one cannot disprove from these data that public financing would have grown even faster or expanded sooner had the option of private financing been denied users of the relevant services. Nevertheless, the data cast doubt on the simple argument that existing levels of funding under the public financing scheme will inevitably be eroded by allowing growth in private financing programs.

In his comprehensive history of Medicare in Canada, Taylor (1987) also documents that the emergence and growth of a publicly-financed health insurance program expanded access to health care within the population. Public financing of health care in Canada can be traced back to the *Rural Municipalities Act* passed in 1909 in Saskatchewan. The Act enabled municipal councils to pass bylaws for the purpose of granting financial relief to any needy person who was a resident of the municipality. In addition to providing hospital care for indigents, a number of municipalities began paying the hospital bills for all their ratepayers and collecting the necessary revenues through the general land tax. In 1934, the Act was amended to empower the council to fix an annual tax for non-ratepayers — the initial granting of statutory authority to levy personal taxes for health services in Canada. A survey conducted in 1944 of 54 municipal hospitalization programs revealed that 12.9 percent of the covered population was hospitalized as compared to 11.7 percent of the general population (Taylor, 1987:93).

Early provincial government hospitalization insurance programs were in some respects of better quality than existing private insurance programs including Blue Cross and commercial coverage programs. For example, Saskatchewan (in 1947) implemented a universal, compulsory hospital care insurance system that provided for an almost complete range of hospital services as benefits at the standard ward level with no limitation on entitlement days as long as in-patient care was "medically necessary". The payment system was also all-inclusive, with no distinction between basic services and the so-called extras then common in Blue Cross and other voluntary or commercial coverage. British Columbia introduced a similar program two years later. By contrast, Blue Cross usually set limits in terms of the numbers of days of coverage for each unrelated illness, while commercial plans set limits in terms of both days and payments per day. Individual contracts were also subjected to waiting periods, to exclusions for pre-existing conditions and to cancellation for over-use and at retirement age.

The government insurance programs also exhibited well established administrative economies of scale compared with relatively high overhead costs associated with private insurance, especially for selling and servicing individual policies. Nevertheless, a comparison across provinces shows that differences across provinces in the rates of increase of hospital operating costs were only weakly related to differences in financing schemes. For example, in 1946, costs per patient day in British Columbia were 24 percent higher than in Ontario. In 1951, after British Columbia had introduced a universal, compulsory hospital care insurance program but before Ontario had, costs per patient day in British Columbia were 20 percent higher than in Ontario (Taylor, 1987:111).

The examples of three other countries might be briefly cited as additional evidence on the impacts of mixed funding systems.

The New Zealand Experience

New Zealand heavily funds hospital care through general taxation but, except with regard to particular categories of patients, depends on direct user payments for most primary care (Blank, 1994). Moreover, since 1938, the gap between the various patient benefits and the charges levied by hospitals has widened progressively, so that by the late 1980s, only about one-half of the average cost in a private medical hospital (including geriatric hospitals) and one-third of that in a private surgical hospital was covered by the state subsidy (Joseph and Flynn, 1988). In the area of geriatric care, patients in private hospitals may qualify via a means test for government subsidies. The majority of medical insurance companies do not cover the cost of geriatric hospital treatment. In contrast, for treatment costs in medical and surgical hospitals, private medical insurance coverage is available from several companies, but no special assistance scheme is in place to subsidize the use of private medical and surgical hospitals by the "means-tested" poor.

Between 1973 and 1984, the number of New Zealanders covered by private insurance (primarily Southern Cross Medical Insurance) increased from 9.6 percent of the country's population to about 35 percent (Joseph and Flynn, 1988). Clearly, demand for private insurance can grow in the face of a pre-existing public insurance scheme, just as the reverse was demonstrated in the preceding section. Critics note, however, that rather than reducing waiting lists for public hospital admission, private hospital growth appears to have increased waiting list numbers. Specifically, critics have noted that districts with private hospitals had, on average, waiting lists double those of districts with no private hospitals. The explanation offered is the practice prevalent among specialist physicians of dividing their time (unequally) between duties in public and private hospitals. In effect, private hospitals were able to bid away the time of specialist physicians sufficiently to reduce the "throughput" in public hospitals. Arguably this phenomenon would be mitigated over time by a growth in supply of specialist physicians.

Another observation is that private hospitals have concentrated on simple, elective surgery, leaving more serious acute conditions and most chronic conditions to the public sector. Thus, critics have also identified the potential for the public sector to be burdened with the role of "supplier of last resort" for expensive conditions. At the same time, supporters of the private sector argue that it is more efficient than the public sector (Joseph and Flynn, 1988). In short, the New Zealand experience highlights the potential for cost burdens to be imposed on the publicly-financed sector by growth of the privately financed sector, at least in the short-run.

The Experience in South Africa

While the South African situation is uniquely complicated by its historical racial policies, criticisms of the public-private financing mix have been raised that are similar to those applied to New Zealand. For example, it has been noted that the public hospitals serve many patients holding private insurance who need urgent care or who require the specialized attention available in certain university-affiliated facilities. In these cases, private medical accounts may be rendered by the attending doctors and charges for rooms and services are made by the hospital authorities; however, while these charges are higher than the income-scaled fee imposed by the public financing scheme, they are lower than the fees charged by private for-profit hospitals and, perhaps below the real cost of the services provided (Naylor, 1988:1155). That is, there is some concern about cross-subsidization going from public to private insurance schemes.

It has also been argued that privately-financed hospitals have bid doctors and nurses away from the publicly financed sector, thereby creating "shortages" in the public sector. It might again be argued that this is essentially a short-run phenomenon, as the long-run supply of medical staff, especially given the potential for physician immigration, is relatively elastic, although it may well be true that public hospitals will have to pay more for medical staff as they lose their position as monopsonistic buyers of such services (Naylor, 1988).

The percentage of the South African population enrolled in a private insurance plan increased from 14.7 percent in 1975 to 19.2 percent in 1985 (Naylor, 1988:1159). As Table 6.2 indicates, whites constitute the overwhelming portion of the population buying private health insurance, again underscoring the significance of income as a determinant of access to private insurance. Nevertheless, while the real growth of expenditures under private insurance plans grew at about five percent per annum per insured person over the period 1975 to 1985, public health expenditures also grew, albeit at a slower rate. The impact of the relative growth of private insurance schemes on the overall efficiency of the health-care sector is apparently a matter for debate. That is, there is no clear evidence that the relative growth of private insurance coverage contributed to reduced overall efficiency of the health-care system.

Table 6.2

Black/White Division in Private Insurance Enrollment Growth in South Africa			
	1975	**1980**	**1985**
Percent of whites covered	74.8	79.1	86.8
Percent of blacks covered	2.6	4.6	7.6
Percentage of population covered	14.7	15.9	19.2

Source: Naylor (1988:1159).

The German Experience

The predominant form of health-care financing in Germany is the payroll tax. Individuals earning less than a minimum threshold salary must belong to the public health system and be insured by it. Those earning above the threshold may be insured by the public health system, but have the option of leaving the public system and obtaining private insurance (or no insurance at all). About 26 percent of the German population is above the income threshold. Of these, approximately one-third obtain private insurance. The apparent reason for the majority of high income earners staying in the public scheme is that the insurance premiums in the private schemes depend upon income and not on health characteristics (Prewo, 1995). In Germany, unlike other European countries with significant private insurance components, once an individual obtains private insurance, she no longer pays anything into the public scheme. The individual cannot opt-back into the public system once having opted-out; however, private insurers cannot drop insurees for becoming bad risks.

Prewo (1995) argues that qualitative differences between publicly and privately-funded health care are small. One minor quality difference is that those insured privately have some choice among surgeons and other specialists, whereas those insured by the public scheme do not. There do not appear to be significant differences in waiting times for treatment, nor in the coverages of public and private systems other than for cosmetic surgery.

Econometric Evidence

In a recent study, Globerman and Vining (1995) evaluate the potential impact of private financing on nominal public health-care budgets. Specifically, they consider whether the growth in public health expenditures as a percentage of total public expenditures over the period 1981-1990 is systematically related to the ratio of private health-care expenditures to total health-care expenditures in the early 1980s for a sample of OECD countries. If a larger private financing role undermines support for the publicly financed scheme, one would expect to observe a negative statistical relationship between the two variables, holding other relevant influences constant. In fact, no relationship is observed. If anything, a larger private financing role in the early 1980s is associated with faster subsequent growth in the ratio of public health care expenditures to total government expenditures.

In another test, Globerman and Vining consider whether medical inflation rates are positively related to the share of private health-care financing in total health-care financing. Holding other possible determinants of medical inflation constant, no statistically significant relationship is found to exist between the two variables of interest when the United States is excluded from the sample of countries. The results suggest that the overall efficiency of the health care sector is not influenced in any important way by the mix of funding, at least over a range of funding mix that characterizes the OECD countries other than the United States.

Summary of the Impacts of a Mixed Financing Regime

Basic consumer theory suggests that if individuals cannot get either the quality or quantity of services that they require because of rationing in the public system (whether this is implicit or explicit), they will seek additional services in the private "market". This raises two questions. Can they effectively be prevented from doing so? If they succeed in purchasing such services, what will be the impact on the publicly financed sector? We believe that the answer to the first question is relatively straightforward. It will be impossible to completely constrain Canadians from availing themselves of at least some privately-provided services. Thus, the real question is where, and in what form, Canadians will engage in private financing. Canadians may wish to purchase some forms of medical care in a private "spot" market (for example MRI scans), but most will want to purchase services that require medical insurance. The real policy issue is whether Canadian governments will mitigate, channel, encourage, or actively discourage this demand.

Probably the most acceptable way to mitigate demand for privately-financed health is explicit rationing in the public system that is based on the "culling" of cost-ineffective treatments. Depending on whether health-care budgets stabilize or decline, and on the rate of medical innovation, this might effectively "choke-off" demand for private insurance. Private financing could be channeled by the delineation of cost-effectiveness league table cut-off points or the seemingly administratively simpler designating of "core" and "non-core" procedures. If the core is defined by some cut-off or cost-effectiveness rule then, of course, cost-effectiveness league tables are exactly equivalent, at least in a static sense, to defining a core (and implicitly a non-core). If they are equivalent, then defining a core is not any more administratively simple than a cost-effectiveness league table — they are the same thing. Alternatively, core can be defined using other than efficiency-related criteria. For reasons already discussed at length in this study, this will be a less preferred outcome. Additionally, as budgets change or new information about effectiveness of treatments becomes available, decision-makers will presumably want to modify resource allocation patterns at the margin. This is obviously much easier to do with the continuous ranking of treatments provided by cost-effectiveness league tables.

The use of cost-effectiveness league tables should improve efficiency. It should also "cull out" some procedures which have value to some individuals even though these procedures are not cost-effective in the public system. This may, or may not, lead to increased private demand for these services. However, to the extent that such culling improves access to services which are more medically valuable for the average individual, it should also increase the commitment of individuals, including those with higher incomes, to continue funding the public system. Given the assumption that, at best, government health budgets are stabilizing (or declining in real terms), and that demographic and technological changes will continue to stimulate growth in demand, one can also expect demand for privately-financed medicine to grow in Canada, notwithstanding improved efficiency in the public sector.

If this is true, governments must decide whether they will oppose it and, if so, with what policies and how strenuously. Since there is privately-financed medicine in Canada now, we are clearly concerned with the issue of "how much more" should be allowed and under what conditions. We identified in an earlier chapter two main concerns about the unrestricted and unregulated growth of privately-financed medicine: (1) publicly-financed schemes might subsidize privately-financed schemes with objectionable efficiency and income distribution consequences, and (2) the growth of privately-financed schemes may ultimately erode the support of higher-income taxpayers for Medicare with a resulting decrease in financing of Medicare. Equally, such growth might lead to higher input prices which leave the public scheme with less command over real medical resources.

The first concern is relatively innocuous. Physical separation of publicly and privately-insured delivery systems is an unnecessarily expensive (but viable) method to mitigate the potential for subsidization. In fact, accounting separations combined with transfer pricing based on incremental costs can effectively mitigate subsidy problems without sacrificing the economies associated with more intensive utilization of the existing publicly-financed infrastructure.[10] It will be tempting for administrators of largely publicly-financed facilities to have the providers to privately-financed patients pay "monopoly" prices for access to those facilities. In our view, the government should discourage this. Such a practice might move higher-income individuals closer to the point of actively rejecting the publicly-financed option entirely.

The second concern, in our view, is potentially more problematic. In this regard, it is useful to recall our earlier discussion which described how publicly-funded schemes have grown in the past alongside relatively extensive privately-financed schemes. It should also be recalled that most countries allow some form of privately-financed health care, and there is no evidence we have seen of a degradation of real public funding for health care that can be directly linked to such private financing. In short, while one cannot dismiss the issue, in our view Canadians should not be overly concerned by it.

Our implicit recommendation that the growth of private insurance not be obstructed by Canadian governments should not be interpreted as motivated by an indifference toward the fate of Medicare. We take it as a given that most Canadians support and value the "traditional" Medicare system. Our recommendation is not intended to challenge this position. The issue is strategic: how best to maintain the bulk of what has been traditional Medicare in a changing environment. Our argument is simple: the risks of not allowing domestic private financing outweigh the risks of allowing it. In this sense, the access of poorer Canadians to health care might be enhanced, not diminished, by privately-financed medicine. As well, and assuming that financial resources for the public system do not decline as a result of increased private financing, the quality of care to poorer Canadians might well increase with fewer demands by wealthier

Canadians on the system.

We recognize, of course, that differences in domestic health care received by wealthier and poorer Canadians will be accentuated by the greater availability of privately-funded alternatives. Any extra-billing alternative also raises more complex concerns about equitable access for poorer Canadians than do alternatives which involve parallel but separate public and private financing schemes. To this extent, we confess to being less sanguine about government tolerance of extra-billing practices; however, it is possible to contemplate circumstances under which extra-billing arrangements contribute to the survival of a comprehensive core set of services financed by Medicare.

CHAPTER SEVEN

Overall Summary and Conclusions

The Canadian health-care system is relatively decentralized compared to many other countries as sub-national governments — provinces — have constitutional responsibility for the delivery of health care. Historically, however, the federal government has had considerable influence on the system, with the result that there has been a high degree of structural uniformity. Federal influence, however, will inevitably decline over the next decade. The federal government will simply not be putting in enough budgetary resources to "leverage" continued uniformity. Our proposals, therefore, are primarily addressed to the provincial government level.

Our recommendations are based on the premise that the health-care system will inevitably become more "mixed". In the Canadian context, this means some increase in the role of private financing. This presents two distinct challenges. First, how should a higher ratio of private financing be integrated into the current system, and how should it be regulated? Second, how should the publicly-funded part of the system be adapted in light of the increase in private financing? For many Canadians the latter question is the more important one so we address it first. We have argued that with constrained public budgets the only real choice is whether rationing will be explicit or implicit, not whether there will be rationing *per se*. Ultimately, the case that explicit rationing is preferable to implicit rationing must depend on whether it can be shown that it is "better" than implicit rationing, in terms of valued social goals. It is difficult to see how implicit rationing is superior in terms of any philosophical positions outlined earlier in this paper. There is no particular reason to believe that implicit rationing will "score" well in terms of Rawlsian or Egalitarian criteria. Explicit rationing, however, may be able to do well in terms of Utilitarian and Pragmatic criteria if it can be shown that total health will be improved. This, in turn, rests on the ability to make the case that explicit rationing can be based on rational criteria. Our extensive review of the use of cost-effectiveness measures and cost-effectiveness league tables in a number of contexts is directly relevant to this question. That evidence *broadly* supports the notion that CEA and CUA could be used to rationally allocate health care in Canada. But these case studies also demonstrate that simply mandating the use of these techniques to allocate resources under present circumstances would not be enough.

The first major set of problems are technical. As we have seen, for CEA and CUA league tables to be effective allocation mechanisms, especially in terms of utilitarian criteria, they must be comprehensive; in other words, they must include all major categories of prevention and treatment. If rankings do not cover all procedures somebody or some body must insert procedures that are not ranked according to CUA into the rankings. While in some cases we may hope or expect that this insertion would be based on some "hunch" as to where the procedure would be ranked if the cost-effectiveness methodology were used, there is clearly no guarantee of this. And, of course, even if a procedure is ranked using such a hunch, it has little credibility compared to the "real thing". Anyway, one can argue on the basis of experience in Oregon and elsewhere that this is unlikely to be the only way that treatments get slotted into the league table. As well as being comprehensive, studies must be well done. If the studies are not well done, any apparent comprehensiveness will be chimerical. We have shown that the evidence suggests that CUA is costly and, even with adequate budgets, difficult to do well. Furthermore, across jurisdictions that have health-relevant similarities, there are significant economies of scale in the production of such studies. In this respect, a multi-jurisdiction, decentralized system, which Canada is tending towards in health care, is less than ideal for the production of good quality studies.

The second set of problems are political. The great disadvantage of explicit rationing is that the rationing mechanism provides information about the allocation of health-care resources around which relatively small (and therefore cohesive) interest groups can form and lobby (this theory of interest group behavior is relatively well known, see Olsen, 1965). These are likely to be situations where a procedure has a low CUA ranking, but where benefits are positive for some definable group. Note that such a definition suggests that many such lobbying groups can be expected to form. There are many procedures where members of some definable group receives *some* benefit from treatment and bears no costs (small groups treat costs, except personal opportunity costs, as being effectively zero in a publicly-funded system, because such costs are spread over the whole population).

In spite of the problems just described, it is our recommendation that the Federal government and provinces acknowledge and encourage the use of cost-effectiveness rankings. The extensive review of global activity shows that tremendous progress is being made in producing standardized studies. Obviously, the Federal government is in the best position to play a part in this international effort. It can also play a valuable role in co-ordinating interprovincial standardization. Provincial governments should not only encourage, but might consider mandating, the participation of health-care suppliers in clinically-based outcome studies. Clearly, such efforts entail financial consequences. In this regard, government funding of the relevant research can be justified by the potentially high social rates-of-return in terms of future resource savings in the publicly- (and privately-) funded health care sectors.

This recommendation is linked to the second issue. We have argued that a rational, efficient public system with clear allocation criteria will reduce the impetus to private financing for core services. But we also believe that the combination of increasing demand and budgetary pressures means that there will be tremendous pressure for governments to allow, if not encourage, an increasing degree of private financing. After extensive review of the theoretical questions and the empirical evidence from a number of countries, we believe that dogmatic government opposition to growth of privately-financed health care is inappropriate, and, indeed, potentially threatening to the preservation of the publicly-funded system. While some legitimate social concerns are raised by private financing, most seem addressable. Even the most problematic form of private finance, that is, extra billing, might be addressable, say, by distributing vouchers for health care to poorer Canadians, thereby assisting them in paying for extra-billed services.

ENDNOTES

CHAPTER ONE

[1] See Feschuk (1995:A1). The B.C. government is moving to outlaw all forms of extra billing in the public health-care system, but it has stopped short of banning a parallel, private system. Under Bill 54, a series of amendments to The Medical and Health Care Services Act, doctors would only be able to charge more than the Medicare rate if they completely opt out of the public system. As well, doctors could no longer charge any extra fees for supplies or use of facilities. Private clinics could still be used, but patients could only be billed for services if the clinics are completely outside of the public system. This would mean that the province would pay no part of the fee. See McInnes (1995:P1, P3).

[2] For evidence on waiting periods for hospital admissions in other countries, see OECD (1994:20).

[3] Variations in waiting times are more pronounced, the more narrowly one defines treatment category (Ramsay and Walker, 1995).

[4] See also the discussion which appeared in the media about the merits of providing Down's Syndrome sufferers with lung transplants. The specific case in point involved a 17 year old male — Terry Urquhart. Mr. Urquhart won a battle with authorities to be put on a waiting list for a lung transplant. Critics argued that the scarce organ should have been used in a patient with prospects for living a longer life than Mr. Urquhart. Initially, those in charge of allocating the organs agreed with them. Supporters called it a moral victory. See Mitchell (1995). The larger issue of whether expected length-of-life should be a criteria for receiving services under a publicly-funded health-care system was not debated in any meaningful policy forum.

CHAPTER TWO

[1] In this and all following discussions, distinctions between public financing through taxation and publicly-mandated financing through social insurance contributions are ignored, although the allocative and distributional impacts of the two sources of financing can differ. For example, taxation-sponsored schemes tend to be more income-progressive than social insurance schemes. The evidence is less clear that the progressivity of the delivery side of health care is related to the nature of public financing (Wagstaff, Van Doorslaer, and Paci, 1994).

[2] Again, it should be acknowledged that the allocative and distributional

implications of alternative private financing arrangements may differ. However, the primary focus here is on the public versus private financing dichotomy.

[3] Examples can be cited where governments have attempted to prohibit government doctors from accepting payment from patients, as well as patients paying private-duty nurses for extra care in public hospitals without apparently significantly diminishing the practices. See OECD (1994:20).

[4] For some New Zealand evidence on this, see Joseph and Flynn (1988). For a discussion of the German experience, see Prewo (1995).

[5] The word "relatively" is stressed, since many countries could still be considered to have implicit allocation criteria.

[6] Some Canadian provinces seem to be drifting towards the UK model.

[7] Mechanic (1992) defends implicit rationing on the grounds that it reduces social divisiveness, as most people will not even realize that doctors are making decisions with rationing criteria in mind.

CHAPTER THREE

[1] Veatch (1982) identifies the theoretical positions described below as comprehensively encompassing the positions that are likely to be taken by participants in the health-care policy debate.

[2] The utilitarian approach is sometimes associated with "producing the greatest good for the greatest number", although the maximization of net social benefits can result in a very concentrated distribution of those net benefits across the population, unless explicit redistribution policies are implemented.

[3] It has also been (critically) noted that changing the standard of care by placing greater weight on economic considerations would alter the fiduciary nature of the physician-patient relationship.

[4] This is not to say that it is a simple rule to implement given the current state of knowledge. Hirschfeld (1992) argues that there is generally agreement on which health-care services will almost certainly yield a benefit for a patient and on what services will almost definitely not be beneficial. However, there is a zone of uncertainty about whether other health-care services will benefit the patient. In a later section, initiatives currently being implemented in various countries to "narrow" this zone of uncertainty are discussed.

[5] In other cases, analysts couch equity objectives in terms of minimum standards rather than in terms of strict equality of access. A review of alternative definitions of equity is provided in Wagstaff, Van Doorslaer and Paci (1994).

[6] A recent high profile case involving a 70 year old Ontario man has

raised suspicion that age is implicitly being used as a rationing criterion in Canada. The individual was told by Ontario doctors that he was "not a candidate for bypass surgery". However, he was given an (apparently successful) coronary bypass surgery in a Texas hospital. The Ontario Ministry of Health is unwilling to pay for the bypass operation and the individual is appealing the decision. Taken as a whole, Canadian incidence rates for cardiac surgery are around 50 percent of those in the U.S., although Canada has higher incidence rates for tonsil, bladder, and appendix surgery (Platiel, 1995).

[7] Moral hazard refers to the reduced incentive that individuals enjoying free health care have to prevent self-inflicted health-care problems.

CHAPTER FOUR

[1] Outcome comparison studies are not discussed here. While this is a closely-related topic, variations among individuals or institutions on outcomes do not directly relate to choosing between procedures or treatments, and therefore do not directly relate to rationing issues. Of course, indirectly they do because the elimination, or retraining of less productive (effective) individuals or institutions can be expected to improve the cost-effectiveness of the whole health system. For one example of this kind of research, see Cleary (1994).

[2] For a discussion of other, less comprehensive techniques, such as cost minimization, see Drummond, Stoddart, and Torrance (1987:7-9 and 39-73).

[3] However, only where budgetary cost happens to exactly equal opportunity cost, *and* the effectiveness measure is the only impact for which people are willing to pay, *and* the scale of the alternatives being compared are the same.

[4] This example is taken from Mooney (1994:10). He also provides detailed criticisms of QALY measures.

[5] Mooney (1994:14). There is no consensus on which method is preferred.

[6] There is considerable evidence that questionnaire respondents are sensitive to how questions are phrased or "framed"; designers of surveys ordinarily try to mitigate the impacts of such sensitivity on the survey results, see Camerer and Kunreuther (1989).

[7] The practical difficulties of actually finding enough (competent) studies is illustrated by Coast (1993).

[8] In the case of the Netherlands, a national debate concerning restrictions on provision of publicly funded health care apparently led to no real choices being made and the basic purchase of covered benefits remaining largely unchanged (HSU 2000, 1994:69).

CHAPTER FIVE

[1] A number of relevant demand studies are reviewed in Phelps (1992).

[2] Parker (1991) reports that most studies fail to identify a relationship between aggregate indicators of health status and expenditures on health care. As a related observation, the Black Report used a variety of morbidity and mortality measures to come to a conclusion that the National Health Service has not significantly affected the disparity between healthier, higher socio-economic groups and less healthy, lower socio-economic groups (see McGuire, Fenn, and Mayhew, 1994:24).

[3] A comprehensive discussion of this and related market failures is found in Evans (1984).

[4] For a preliminary empirical assessment of the relevant dynamics, see Globerman and Vining (1995). Also, see Besley and Gouveia (1994).

[5] We are assuming here that buying services in the private sector does not relieve the individual of the tax burden to finance publicly-funded insurance. In this context, we envision regimes such as those in the United Kingdom and France where private insurance is supplemental and doesn't free the privately insured from paying taxes that support the public health-care system, nor from paying the premium to the public system. Conversely, the German system allows for "opting out". That is, when individuals pay a premium to a private health insurance company, they no longer pay anything into the public system. For a description of the German system, see Prewo (1995).

[6] In a related version of this argument, "high quality" physicians and other professionals are bid away from the public sector to the private sector.

[7] An identification of the types of innovations that might be stimulated by competition among third-party payers of health-care expenditures is provided in Glennerster and Matsaganis (1993). For a broader discussion of the potential advantages (and disadvantages) of a diversity of insurance plans, see Aaron (1991).

[8] For a comprehensive literature review, see McFetridge and Corvari (1985).

[9] This is not strictly speaking increased competition from private insurers. Rather, it can be seen as increased competition within the publicly-financed sector.

[10] On the other hand, Aaron (1991) asserts that the increased administrative and transaction costs associated with multiple insurers are substantial.

[11] Equivalently, healthy individuals who can "opt-out" of the public system may be able to obtain lower insurance rates in the private sector,

particularly if they are high-income earners. As noted earlier, we do not consider the case where individuals can simply opt-out of the public system as individual taxpayers.

[12] As a case in point, Glennerster and Matsaganis (1993) note that the budgets provided general practitioner fundholders in the United Kingdom initially covered only standard, relatively inexpensive treatment without open-ended treatment following on. Furthermore, practices were told that if any patient cost them more than £5,000 the district health authority would pick up the bill.

[13] Canada's Minister of Health in March 1995 issued an ultimatum to the provinces to stop funding private health clinics that charge patients extra fees. Her argument was that it violated the Canada Health Act by making some "essential" services less accessible to those who can't afford private clinics. Some have interpreted her position as being that she is not against private clinics, *per se*, but against public subsidy of private clinics (see the *Globe and Mail*, March 3, 1995:A2).

[14] For a discussion of this and other issues related to competition between independent and integrated telephone companies, see Globerman, Janisch and Stanbury (1995).

[15] This pricing rule is extensively discussed in W.J. Baumol and J.G. Sidak (1994).

[16] The point to emphasize here is that much of the purchasing of private insurance will be to supplement rather than replace use of the public system. In this regard, extra-billing arrangements are less likely to trigger "defections" from the public system than arrangements where complete private financing is required.

[17] Quality differences across service providers can be mitigated by increased government efforts to monitor performance and publicize the results of performance monitoring. Where it is not possible, for one reason or another, to pay "high quality" suppliers more than "low quality" suppliers under the public insurance scheme, extra-billing is a way for high quality suppliers to earn more income, at the margin. This makes it more likely that high quality suppliers will remain working for the public insurance scheme.

[18] In this respect, current policies to restrict the growth of trained healthcare personnel are perverse.

CHAPTER SIX

[1] It was noted by the OECD (1994:17) that Canada is the only country it studied which, since 1984, made no charges for medical services covered by Federal Law. This publication reports the wide variation across

OECD countries in cost-sharing for health-care services.

[2] Different types of private health-care financing schemes are discussed in Besley and Gouveia (1994).

[3] See Gray (1994:234). The following discussion of the British inter-war experience is based largely upon this reference.

[4] A similar discussion is found in Reekie (1995).

[5] Aaron (1991) cites the community rating practices of Blue Cross and Blue Shield as creating an analogy to public insurance schemes. He notes that competition from private insurers ultimately led Blue Cross and Blue Shield to adopt experience rating practices.

[6] This assessment is increasingly dated by the emergence and growth of HMO-type insurers and the like.

[7] Rivers and Mobley (1992) concludes that increased competition in California health insurance markets has probably contributed to substantial price-based competition among hospitals reflected in contracting rates in excess of 30 percent or more in some hospitals.

[8] We referenced earlier evidence for Great Britain that differences in health status exist across socio-economic groups, notwithstanding universal government health insurance. Hall (1993) investigated the change in health status over time following the introduction of medicare in Australia in 1984. She found no evidence to suggest that the introduction of medicare led to any increase in the health of the previously uninsured.

[9] The seminal historical discussion of the Canadian Medicare System is provided by Taylor (1987) upon which most of the following discussion is based.

[10] Admittedly, there will be some additional administrative cost burden introduced.

REFERENCES

Aaron, H., *Serious and Unstable Condition* (Washington, D.C.: The Brookings Institution, 1991).

Abel-Smith, B. and E. Mossiados, "Cost Containment and Health Care Reform: A Study of the European Union", *Health Policy*, Vol. 28, 1994, pp. 89-132.

Abel-Smith, B., *Value for Money in Health Services* (London: Heinemann, 1981).

Antonanzas, F., R. Garuz, J. Rovira, F. Anton, C. Trinxet, E. Navas, and L. Salleras, "Cost-Effectiveness of Hepatitis Vaccination Strategies in Catalonia, Spain", *PharmacoEconomics*, Vol. 7, No. 5, 1995, pp. 428-443.

Appleby, T., "Safety Net Stretches Wide and Thin", *The Globe and Mail,* July 22, 1994, A8.

Arevalo, J.A. and A.E. Washington, "Cost-Effectiveness of Prenatal Screening and Immunization for Hepatitis B Virus", *Journal of American Medical Association*, Vol. 259, 1988, pp. 771-774.

Armstrong, D., J. Fry, and P. Armstrong, "General Practitioners' Views of Clinical Guidelines for the Management of Asthma", *International Journal for Quality in Health Care*, Vol. 6, No. 2, 1994, pp. 199-202.

Baumol, W., "Macroeconomics of Unbalanced Growth: The Anatomy of Urban Crisis", *American Economic Review,* Vol. 57, 1967, pp. 415-426.

Baumol, W.J. and J.G. Sidak, *Toward Competition in Local Telephony* (Cambridge, MA: MIT Press and American Enterprise Institute, 1994).

Baumol, W., S. Bateman, and E. Wolff, *Productivity and American Leadership: The Long View* (Cambridge, Mass: The MIT Press, 1989).

Besley, T. and M. Gouveia, "Alternative Systems of Health Care Provisions", *Economic Policy*, Vol. 19, October, 1994, pp. 200-258.

Birch, S. and A. Gafni, "Cost Effectiveness Ratios: In a League of their Own", *Health Policy*, Vol. 28, No. 2, May 1994, pp. 133-141.

Blank, R., "Regulatory Rationing: A Solution to Health Care Resource Allocation", *University of Pennsylvania Law Review,* Vol. 40, 1992, pp. 1573-1596.

Blank, R., *Rationing Medicine* (New York: Columbia University Press, 1988).

Bloom, B., A. Hillman, M. Fendrick, and J.S. Schwartz, "A Reappraisal of Hepatitis B Virus Vaccination Strategies Using Cost-Effectiveness Analysis", *Annals of Internal Medicine*, Vol. 18, No. 4, 1993, pp. 298-307.

Blumstein, J. and F. Sloan, *Organ Transplant Policy* (Durham, N.C.:

Duke University Press, 1989).

Boardman, A., W. Mallery, and A. Vining, "Learning from Ex Ante/Ex Post Cost-Benefit Comparisons: The Coquihalla Highway Example", *Socio-Economic Planning Sciences*, Vol. 28, No. 2, 1994, pp. 69-84.

Boothe, P. and B. Johnston, *Stealing the Emperor's Clothes: Deficit Offloading and National Standards in Health Care*, C.D. Howe Institute Commentary 41 (Toronto: C.D. Howe Institute, 1993).

Bridgport Group, "The Core Debate: Stage One: How We Define the Core: Review of Submissions", Department of Health, Wellington, N.Z., 1992.

Calabrisi, P. and G. Bobbitt, *Tragic Choices*, (New York: Norton, 1978).

Callahan, D., *Setting Limits: Medical Goals in an Aging Society* (New York: Simon and Schuster, 1987).

Camerer, C. and H. Kunreuther, "Decision Processes for Low Probability Events: Policy Implications", *Journal of Policy Analysis and Management*, Vol. 8, No. 4, 1989, pp.565-592.

Carrrere, M., "The Reaction of Private Physicians to Price Deregulation in France", *Social Science and Medicine,* Vol. 33, No. 11, 1991, pp. 1221-1228.

Cernetig, M., "Ottawa accused of ruining Medicare", *The Globe and Mail*, April 12, 1995, A1, A5.

Chassim, M., J. Kosecoff, R. Park, C. Winslow, K. Kahn, N. Merrick, J. Kesseo, A. Funk, D. Solomon, and R. Brook, "Does Inappropriate Use Explain Geographic Variation in the Use of Health Care Services?", *Journal of the American Medical Association*, Vol. 258, 1987, p. 2533.

Cleary, R., "Establishing Inter-Hospital Comparisons of Outcomes", *International Journal for Quality in Health Care,* Vol. 6, No. 1, 1994, pp. 31-36.

Coast, J., "The Role of Economic Evaluation in Setting Priorities for Elective Surgery", *Health Policy*, Vol. 24, 1993, pp. 243-257.

Courchene, T., *Social Canada in the Millenium* (Toronto, Ont.: C.D. Howe, 1994).

Coutts, J., "Health care resists European cure", *The Globe and Mail*, March 8, 1995, A5.

Crichton, A., D. Hsu, and S. Tsang, *Canada's Health-care System: Its Funding and Organization* (Ottawa, Ont.: CHA Press, 1994).

Cumming, J., "Core Services and Priority-Setting: The New Zealand Experience", *Health Policy*, Vol. 29, No. 1, 2, July/August 1994, pp. 41-60.

Currie, J. and D. Thomas, "Medical Care for Children: Public Insurance, Private Insurance and Racial Differences in Utilization", *The Journal of Human Resources*, Vol. XXX, No. 1, Winter 1995, pp. 135-162.

Cyert, R. and J. March, *Behavioral Theory of the Firm* (Englewood Cliffs, N.J.: Prentice-Hall, 1963).

Daniels, N., "Is the Oregon Rationing Plan Fair?", *Journal of the American Medical Association*, Vol. 265, No. 17, May 1, 1991, pp. 2232-2235.

Deber, R., S. Mhatre, and G. Baker, "A Review of Provincial Initiatives", pp. 91-124, in A. Blomqvist and D. Brown, eds., *Limits to Care* (Toronto: C.D. Howe Institute, 1994).

Demicheli, V. and T.O. Jefferson, "Cost-Benefit Analysis of the Introduction of Mass Vaccination Against Hepatitis B in Italy", *Journal of Public Health Medicine*, Vol. 14, No. 4, December 1992, pp. 367-375.

Digby, A. and N. Bosanquet, "Doctors and Patients in an Era of National Health Insurance and Private Practice, 1913-1938", *Economic History Review*, 2nd series, Vol. XLI, No. 1, 1988, pp. 74-94.

Donabedian, A., *The Criteria and Standards of Quality* (Ann Arbor, MI: Health Administration Press, 1982).

Drummond, M., A. Brandt, B. Luce, and J. Rovira, "Standardizing Economic Evaluation Methodologies in Health Care: Practice, Problems and Potential", *International Journal of Technology Assessment in Health Care*, Vol. 9, No. 1, 1993, pp. 26-36.

Drummond, M., D. Hailey, and C. Selby-Smith, "Maximizing the Impact of Health Technology Assessment: The Australian Case", in C. Selbey-Smith, *Economics and Health*, Proceedings of the 13th Australian Conference on Health Economics, Public Sector Management Institute, Monash University, 1992.

Drummond, M., G.L. Stoddart, and G.W. Torrance, *Methods for the Economic Evaluations of Health-care Programmes* (Oxford: Oxford University Press, 1987).

Drummond, M.F., J.M. Mason, and G.W. Torrance, "Cost-Effectiveness League Tables: More Harm than Good?", *Social Science and Medicine*, Vol. 37, No. 1, July 1993, pp. 33-40.

Dubois, R., "Reducing Unnecessary Care: Different Approaches to the 'Big Ticket' and the 'Little Ticket' Items", *Journal of Ambulatory Care Management*, Vol. 14, No. 4, October 1991, p. 30-37.

Durenberger, D. and S.B. Foote, "Medical Technology Meets Managed Competition", *Journal of American Health Policy*, May/June 1993, pp. 23-31.

Edelson, J., M. Weinstein, A. Tosteson, A. Williams, L. Lee, and L. Goldman, "Long-Term Cost-Effectiveness of Various Initial Monotherapies for Mild to Moderate Hypertension", *Journal of the American Medical Association*, Vol. 263, No. 3, January 1990, pp.

407-413.

Evans, R., R.G. Evans, J. Lomas, M.L. Barer, R.J. Labelle, C. Fooks, G.L. Stoddard, G.M. Anderson, D. Feeny, A. Gafni, G. W. Torrance, and W.G. Tholl, "Controlling Health Expenditures — The Canadian Reality", *The New England Journal of Medicine*, Vol. 320, No. 9, 1989, pp. 571-577.

Evans, R., M. Barer, G. Stoddart, and V. Bhatia, "It's Not the Money, It's the Principle: Why User Charges for Some Services and Not Others?", Toronto: The Premier's Council on Health, Well-Being and Social Justice Discussion Paper, 1994.

Evans, R., *Strained Mercy: The Economics of Canadian Health Care* (Toronto: Butterworth, 1984).

Feschuk, S., "PM rejects Klein's Medicare ideas", *The Globe and Mail*, April 14, 1995, A1.

Field, M. and K. Lohr, Institute of Medicine, *Guidelines for Clinical Practice: From Development to Use* (Washington, D.C.: National Academy Press, 1992).

Fox, D.M., "The Once and Future Payers of Last Resort: The States and AIDs", pp. 24-48, in H.M. Leichter, ed., *Health Policy Reform in America: Innovations from the States* (Armonk, New York: ME Sharpe Inc., 1992).

Frazier, H. and F. Mosteller, *Medicine Worth Paying For: Assessing Medical Innovations* (Cambridge, MA: Harvard University Press, 1995).

Froberg, D. and R.L. Kane, "Methodology for Measuring Health-State Preferences — IV: Progress and a Research Agenda", *Journal of Clinical Epidemiology*, Vol. 42, No. 7, 1989, pp. 675-685.

Gafni, A., "Time in Health: Can We Measure Individuals' Pure Time Preference?", *Medical Decision Making*, Vol. 15, No. 1, 1995, pp. 31-37.

Gerard, K. and G. Mooney, "QALY League Tables: Three Points for Concern — Goal Difference Counts", Health Economics Research Unit Discussion Paper No. 04-92, University of Aberdeen, 1992.

Gerard, K., "Cost-Utility in Practice: A Policy Maker's Guide to the State of the Art", *Health Policy*, Vol. 21, No. 3, 1992, pp. 249-279.

Gerard, K., "Setting Priorities in the New NHS: Can Purchasers Use Cost-Utility Information?", *Health Policy*, Vol. 25, Nos. 1, 2, September 1993, pp. 109-25.

Glaser, W., *Health Insurance in Practice* (San Francisco: Jossey-Bass Publishers, 1991).

Glennerster, H. and M. Matsaganis, "The UK Reforms: The Fund-holding Experiment", *Health Policy*, Vol. 23, No.3, March 1993, pp. 179-191.

Globerman, S. and A. Vining, "A Framework for Evaluating the Government Contracting-Out Decision with an Application to Information Technology", forthcoming in *Public Administration Review*, 1996.

Globerman, S., H. Janisch, and W.T. Stanbury, "Analysis of Telecom Decision 94-19, Review of Regulatory Framework", pp. 417-440, in S. Globerman, W.T. Stanbury, and T. Wilson, eds., *The Future of Telecommunications Policy in Canada* (Vancouver: University of British Columbia, Bureau of Applied Research, 1995).

Goldberg, L. and W. Greenberg, "The Competitive Response of Blue Cross to the Health Maintenance Organization", *Economic Inquiry*, Vol. XVIII, 1980, pp. 55-68.

Goldberg, L. and W. Greenberg, "The Determinants of HMO Enrollment and Growth", *Health Services Research*, Vol. 16, No. 4, Winter 1981, pp. 421-438.

Goldberg, L. and W. Greenberg, "The Response of the Dominant Firm to Competition: The Ocean State Case", *Health Care Management Review*, Vol. 20, No. 1, 1995, pp. 65-74.

Gray, A.M., "A Mixed Economy of Health Care: Britain's Health Service Sector in the Inter-War Period", in McGuire, Fenn, and Mayher, pp. 233-260.

Greenspon, E., "Social cuts deep; old-age review next", *The Globe and Mail*, February 28, 1995, A1.

Hadorn, D., "The Oregon Priority-Setting Exercise: Cost-Effectiveness and the Rule of Rescue, Revisited", *Medical Decision Making*, Vol. 16, No. 2, 1996, pp. 117-119.

Hadorn, D., "Health-care Effectiveness Research and Public Policy", unpublished paper, 1988.

Hall, J., "Equity in Health Care", Ph.D. thesis, Department of Public Health, University of Sydney, Sydney, 1993.

Hausman, J.A., *Contingent Valuation: A Critical Assessment* (N.Y.: North-Holland, 1993).

Hay, J.W. and J.J. Leahy, "Competition Among Health Plans: Some Preliminary Evidence", *Southern Economic Journal*, Vol. 50, No. 3, 1984, pp. 831-846.

Hayward, R., M. Shapiro, H. Freeman, and C. Corey, "Inequities in Health Services Among Insured Americans", *New England Journal of Medicine*, Vol. 318, No. 23, June 9, 1988, pp. 1507-1512.

Health and Welfare Canada, *Health Expenditures in Canada: Fact Sheets* (Ottawa: Policy, Planning and Information Branch, Health and Welfare Canada, 1993).

Health and Welfare Canada, *Provincial and Territorial Drug*

Reimbursement Programs: Descriptive Summary, (Ottawa: Policy, Planning and Information Branch, Health and Welfare Canada, 1990).

Heikkila, E. and R.S. Luo, "A Note on Public Versus Private Provision of Substitutable Yet Exclusively Provided Goods", University of Southern California, School of Urban and Regional Planning, mimeo, October 1994.

Hornberger, J.C., D.A. Redelmeier, and J. Peterson, "Variability Among Methods to Assess Patients' Well-Being and Consequent Effect on a Cost-Effectiveness Analysis", *Journal of Clinical Epidemiology*, Vol. 45, No. 5, 1992, pp. 505-512.

HSU 2000, *International Perspectives on Healthcare Reform in Sweden*, (Stockholm: Ministry of Health and Social Affairs, 1994).

Hurst, J., *The Reform of Health Care — A Comparative Analysis of Seven OECD Countries*, Health Policy Studies, No. 2, Paris: OECD, 1995.

Institute of Medicine, *Assessing Medical Technologies* (Washington, D.C.: National Academy Press, 1985).

Johannesson, M. and B. Jonsonn, "Cost-Effectiveness Analysis of Hypertension Treatment: A Review of Methodological Issues", *Health Policy*, Vol. 19, No. 1, September, 1991, pp. 55-78.

Johannesson, M., J. Pliskin, and M. Weinstein, "A Note on QALYs, Time Tradeoff and Discounting", *Medical Decision Making*, Vol. 14, No. 2, 1994, pp. 188-193.

Jones-Lee, M.W., *The Economics of Safety and Physical Risk* (Oxford: Basil Blackwell, 1989).

Joseph, A. and H. Flynn, "Regional and Welfare Perspectives on the Public-Private Hospital Dichotomy in New Zealand", *Social Science and Medicine*, Vol. 26, No. 1, 1988, pp. 101-110.

Kaplan, R.M., "Value Judgement in the Oregon Medical Experiment", *Medical Care*, Vol. 32, No. 10, 1994, pp. 975-988.

Kawachi, I. and L. Malcolm, "The Cost-Effectiveness of Various Initial Monotherapies for Mild to Moderate Hypertension", *Journal of Hypertension*, Vol. 9, No. 3, March, 1991, pp. 199-208.

Keeler, E.B. and S. Critin, "Discounting of Life-Saving and Other Non-Monetary Effects", *Management Science*, Vol. 29, No. 1983, pp. 300-306.

Kind, P., R. Rosser, and A. Williams, "Valuation of Quality of Life: Some Psychometric Evidence", pp. 159-170, in M.W. Jones-Lee, *The Value of Life and Safety* (Amsterdam: Elsevier/North Holland, 1982).

Kinosian, B.P. and J.M. Eisenberg, "Cutting into Cholesterol: Cost-Effective Alternatives for Treating Hypercholesterolemia", *Journal of the American Medical Association*, Vol. 258, 1988, pp. 2249-2254.

Kirkman-Liff, B., "Health Care Reform in the Netherlands, Germany and the United Kingdom", in A. Blomqvist and D. Brown, eds., op. cit., pp. 167-216.

Klein, R., "Can We Restrict the Health Care Menu?", *Health Policy*, Vol. 27, No.2, February,1994, pp. 103-112.

Krahn, M. and A. Detsky, "Should Canada and the United States Universally Vaccinate Infants Against Hepatitis B?", *Medical Decision Making*, Vol. 13, No. 1, 1993, pp. 4-20.

Kristiansen, I.S., A. Eggen, and D. Thelle, "Cost Effectiveness of Incremental Programmes for Lowering Serum Cholesterol Concentration: Is Individual Intervention Worthwhile?", *British Medical Journal*, Vol. 302, No. 6785, 1991, pp. 1119-1122.

Lamm, R.D., "Rationing of Health Care: Inevitable and Desirable", *University of Pennsylvania Law Review*, Vol. 140, No. 5, May, 1992, pp. 1511-1523.

LaPuma, J. and E. Lawlor, "Quality-Adjusted Life Years: Ethical Implications for Clinicians and Policymakers", *Journal of the American Medical Association*, Vol. 263, No. 21, June 6, 1990, p. 2917-2921.

LeGrand, J., *The Strategy of Equality* (London: Allen and Unwin, 1982).

Lewis, D., "The Provision of Dental Care in Canada", pp. 313-328, in B. Burt and S. Eckland, eds., *Dentistry, Dental Practice and the Community* (Philadelphia: W.B. Saunders Co., 1992).

Lewis, S., "Quality, Context and Distributive Justice: The Role of Utilization Research and Management", *International Journal of Quality in Health Care*, Vol. 7, No. 4, 1995, pp. 325-331.

Liberati, A., G. Apolone, T. Lang, and S. Lorenzo, "A European Project Assessing the Appropriateness of Hospital Utilization: Background, Objectives and Preliminary Results", *International Journal for Quality in Health Care*, Vol. 7, No. 3, 1995, pp. 187-199.

Lohr, K., "Guidelines for Clinical Practice: Applications for Primary Care", *International Journal for Quality in Health Care*, Vol. 6, No. 1, 1994, pp. 17-25.

Loomes, G. and L. McKenzie, "The Use of QALYs in Health Care Decision Making", *Social Science and Medicine*, Vol. 24, No. 4, 1989, pp. 299-308.

Marmor, T. and J. Blumstein, "Introduction to Rationing", *University of Pennsylvania Law Review*, Vol. 141, 1992, pp. 1539-1542.

Martens, L.L., F.F. Rutten, D.W. Erkelens, *et. al.*, "Cost-Effectiveness of Cholesterol-Lowering Therapy in the Netherlands", *American Journal of Medicine*, Vol. 87, October 16, 1989, Supplement 4A, pp. 54S-58S.

Marzouk, M.S., "Aging, Age-Specific Health Care Costs and the Future Health Care Burden in Canada", *Canadian Public Policy*, Vol. XVII,

No. 4, 1991, pp. 490-505.

Mason, J.M., M.F. Drummond, and G.W. Torrance, "Some Guidelines on the Use of Cost-Effectiveness League Tables", *British Medical Journal*, Vol. 306, 1993, pp. 570-572.

Maynard, A., "Developing the Health-care Market", *Economic Journal*, Vol. 101, 1991, pp. 1277-1286.

McFetridge, D. and R.J. Corvari, "Technology Diffusion: A Survey of Canadian Evidence and Public Policy Issues", pp.177-231, in D.G. McFetridge, ed., *Technological Change in Canadian Industry* (Toronto: University of Toronto Press, 1985).

McGuire, A., P. Fenn, and K. Mayhew, "The Economics of Health Care", pp. 233-260, in A. McGuire, P. Fenn, and K. Mayhew, *Providing Health Care: The Economics of Alternative Systems of Finance and Delivery* (Oxford: Oxford University Press, 1994).

McInnes, C., "B.C. won't outlaw private health care", *The Globe and Mail*, June 30, 1995, P1, P3.

Mendelson, D., R. Abramson, and R. Rubin, "State Involvement in Medical Technology Assessment", *Health Affairs*, Vol. 14, No. 2, Summer 1995, pp. 83-98.

Mhatre, S. and R. Deber, "From Equal Access to Health Care to Equitable Access to Health: A Review of Canadian Provincial Health Commissions and Reports", *International Journal of Health Services*, Vol. 22, Number 4, 1992, pp. 645-668.

Mickleburg, R., "Private Firms Seek to Fill Gaps in Health Coverage", *The Globe and Mail*, May 7, 1994, A4.

Miller, M., J. Holahan, and W.P. Welch, "Geographic Variations in Physician Service Utilization", *Medical Care Research and Review*, Vol. 52, No. 2, 1995, pp. 252-278.

Mitchell, A., "Down's transplant bid poses dilemma", *The Globe and Mail*.

Mooney, G., *Key Issues in Health Economics* (New York: Harvester Wheatsheaf, 1994).

Morrall, III, J.F., "Controlling Regulatory Costs: The Use of Regulatory Budgeting", OECD Public Management Occasional Papers, Regulatory Management and Reform Series, No. 2, Paris, 1992.

Mosteller, F. and H. Frazier, "Evaluating Medical Technologies", Ch. 2 in H. Frazier and F. Mosteller, 1995.

Mosteller, F. and H. Frazier, "Improving the Health Care System", Ch. 17 in H. Frazier and F. Mosteller, 1995.

Mueller, D., *Public Choice II*, (Cambridge: Cambridge University Press, 1989).

Mujinja, P., Urassa, D., and Mnyika, K., "The Tanzanian Public/Private

Mix in National Health Care", Paper for the Workshop on the Public/ Private Mix, London: LSHTM, January, 1993.

Naylor, C., G. Anderson, and V. Goel, eds., *Patterns of Health Care in Ontario* (Ottawa: Canadian Medical Association, 1994).

Naylor, D., "Private Medicine and the Privatization of Health Care in South Africa", *Social Science and Medicine*, Vol. 27, No. 11, 1988, pp. 1153-1170

Neumann, J. and M. Johannesson, "The Willingness to Pay for In Vitro Fertilization: A Pilot Study Using Contingent Valuation", *Medicare Care*, Vol. 32, No. 7, 1994, pp. 686-699.

Neumann, P.J. and M. Johannesson, "From Principle to Public Policy: Using Cost-Effectiveness Analysis", *Health Affairs*, Vol. 13, No. 3, 1994, pp. 206-214.

Newhouse, J. and the Insurance Experiment Group, *Free for All? Lessons from the RAND Health Experiment* (Cambridge, Mass.: Harvard University Press, 1993).

Nord, E., "The Validity of a Visual Scale in Determining Social Utility Weights for Health States", *Journal of Health Planning and Management*, Vol. 6, 1991, pp. 234-242.

Nord, E., "Unjustified Use of the Quality of Well-Being Scale in Priority Setting in Oregon", *Health Policy*, Vol. 24, No. 1, April, 1993, pp. 45-53.

OECD, *New Directions in Health-care Policy* (Paris: OECD, 1995).

OECD, *OECD Health Data* (Paris: OECD, 1993).

OECD, *OECD Health Systems: Facts and Trends 1960-1991*, Volume 1 (Paris: OECD, 1993).

OECD, *The Reform of Health-care Systems: A Review of Seventeen OECD Countries* (Paris: OECD, 1994).

Paccaud, F. and H. Guillain, "Should We Assess Appropriateness of Care in Europe?", *International Journal for Quality in Health Care*, Vol. 6, No. 3, 1994, pp. 239-243.

Pauly, M., "Producing Research on Health Management and Managed Care: Market Failure or Market Success?", *Medical Care Research and Review*, Vol. 53, Supplement March 1996, pp. S.118-131.

Phelps, C.E. and S.T. Parente, "Priority Setting in Medical Technology and Medical Practice Assessment", *Medical Care*, Vol. 28, No. 8, August 1990, pp. 703-723.

Phelps, C.E., *Health Economics* (New York: Harper Collins Publishers Inc., 1992).

Platiel, R., "The Age Factor in Heart Surgery", *The Globe and Mail*, June 2, 1995, A9.

Prewo, W., "Two-Tiered Health Care: The Case of Germany", *Fraser*

Forum, October 1995, pp. 5-12.

Ramsay, C. and M. Walker, *Waiting Your Turn: Hospital Waiting Lists in Canada* (5th Edition), (Vancouver: The Fraser Institute, 1995).

Rawls, J., *A Theory of Justice* (Cambridge, MA: Harvard University Press, 1971).

Redelmeier, D.A., D.N. Heller, and C. Weinstein, "Time Preference in Medical Economics: Science or Religion?", *Medical Decision Making*, Vol. 14, No. 3, 1994, pp. 301-303.

Reekie, D., *Government in Health Care: Lessons from the U.K.* (Hayward: Smith Center for Private Enterprise Studies, 1995).

Restuccia, J.D., "The Evolution of Hospital Utilization Review Methods in the United States", *International Journal for Quality in Health Care*, Vol. 17, No. 3, 1995, pp. 253-260.

Rivers-Mobley, L., "The Behavior of Multihospital Chains in Increasingly Competitive California Hospital Markets", in Richard M. Scheffler and Louis F. Rossiter, eds., *Advances in Health Economics and Health Services Research* (Greenwich, Conn.: JAI Press, 1992), pp. 165-190.

Ross, J., "The Use of Economic Evaluation in Health Care: Australian Decision Makers' Perceptions", *Health Policy*, Vol. 31, No. 2, February 1995, pp. 103-110.

Sackett, D.L. and G.W. Torrance, "The Utility of Different Health States as Perceived by the General Public", *Journal of Chronic Diseases*, Vol. 31, No. 11, 1978, pp. 697-704.

Salkeld, G., P. Davey, and G. Arnolda, "A Critical Review of Health-Related Economic Evaluations in Australia: Implications for Health Policy", *Health Policy*, Vol. 31, No. 2, February 1995, pp. 111-125.

Schulman, K., B. Kinosian, T.A. Jacobson, *et. al.*, "Reducing High Blood Cholesterol Level with Drugs", *Journal of American Medical Association*, Vol. 264, No. 23, December 19, 1990, pp. 3025-3033.

Schwindt, R. and A. Vining, "Proposal for a Future Delivery Market for Transplant Organs", *Journal of Health Politics, Policy and Law*, Vol. 11, No. 3, 1986, pp. 483-500.

Simon, H., *Administrative Behavior* (2nd edition) (New York: MacMillan, 1957).

Smith, R., "Where is the Wisdom?", *British Medical Journal*, Vol. 303, 1992, pp. 797-799.

Stamm, J., M. Waller, D. Lewis, and G. Stoddart, *Dental Care Reforms in Canada: Historical Developments, Current Status and Future Directions* (Ottawa: Ministry of Supply and Service, 1986).

Stoddart, G., M. Barer, R. Evans, and V. Bhatai, "Why Not User Charges? The Real Issues", Discussion Paper prepared for The Premier's Council on Health, Well-Being and Social Justice, September 1993.

Stodgill, R., "Adam Smith to the ER", *Business Week*, June 12, 1995, pp. 64-65.

Swartz, D., "The Politics of Reform: Public Health Insurance in Canada", *International Journal of Health Services,* Vol. 23, No. 2, 1993, pp. 219-238.

Taylor, M., *Health Insurance and Canadian Public Policy* (2nd edition) (Kingston and Montreal: McGill-Queen's University Press, 1987).

Tengs, T. G. Meyer, J. Siegel, J. Pliskin, J. Graham, and M. Weinstein, "Oregon's Medicaid Ranking and Cost-Effectiveness: Is There any Relationship?", *Medical Decision Making*, Vol. 16, No. 2, 1996, pp. 99-107.

Tengs, T., M. Adams, J. Pliskin, *et. al.*, "Five Hundred Life-Saving Interventions and Their Cost-Effectiveness", *Risk Analysis*, Vol. 15, 1995, pp. 369-390.

Tholl, W., "Health Care in Canada: Skating Faster on Thinner Ice", pp. 53-89, in A. Blomqvist and D. Brown, eds., *Limits to Care* (Toronto: C.D. Howe Institute, 1994).

Thorne, J., B. Bianchi, G. Bonnyman, C. Greene, and T. Leddy, "State Perspectives on Health Care Reform: Oregon, Hawaii, Tennessee, and Rhode Island", *Health Care Financing Review*, Vol. 16, No. 3, 1995, pp. 121-138.

Torrance, G.W., M.H. Boyle, and S.P. Horwood, "Application of Multi-Attribute Utility Theory to Measure Social Preferences for Health Status", *Operations Research*, Vol. 30, No. 6, 1982, pp. 1043-1069.

Tullock, G., "The Cost of Medical Progress", *American Economic Review Papers and Proceedings*, Vol. 85, No. 2, 1995, pp. 77-81.

Tuohy, C., "Health Policy and Fiscal Federalism", in K. Banting, D. Brown and T. Courchene, *The Future of Fiscal Federalism* (Kingston, Ont.: School of Policy Studies, Queen's University, 1994).

Tuohy, C., "What Drives Changes in Health Care Policy: A Comparative Perspective", The Timlin Lecture, January 30, 1995, University of Saskatchewan.

Ubel, P., G. Loewenstein, D. Scanlon, and M. Kamlet, "Individual Utilities are Inconsistent with Rationing Choices: A Partial Explanation of Why Oregon's Cost-Effectiveness List Failed", *Medical Decision Making*, Vol. 16, No. 2, 1996, pp.108-116.

Valpy, M., "Health Care Under the Knife", *The Globe and Mail*, February 7, 1996, A23.

Veatch, R.M., "Ethical Dimensions of the Distribution of Health Care", in J. van der Gaag and T. Tsukahara, Jr., *Economics of Health Care* (New York: Praeger Publishers, 1982).

Vining, A.R. and D. Weimer, "Government Supply and Government

Production Failure: A Framework Based on Contestability", *Journal of Public Policy*, Vol. 10, Part 1, 1990, pp. 1-22.

Viscusi, W.K., "The Value of Risks to Life and Health", *Journal of Economic Literature*, Vol. 31, No. 4, 1993, pp. 1912-1946.

Wagstaff, A. and E. Van Doorslaer, "Equity in the Financing of Health Care: Some International Comparisons", *Journal of Health Economics*, Vol. 11, No. 4, 1992, pp. 361-387.

Wagstaff, A., E. Van Doorslaer, and P. Paci, "Equity in the Finance and Delivery of Health Care: Some Tentative Cross-Country Comparisons", in McGuire *et. al.*, 1994, pp. 141-171.

Wennberg, J., "Population Illness Rates do not Explain Population Hospitalization Rates", *Medical Care*, Vol. 25, No. 4, April 1987, pp. 354-359.

Wennberg, J.E., "Dealing with Medical Practice Variations: A Proposal for Action", *Health Affairs*, Vol. 3, No. 7, 1984.

Whittington, D. and D. MacRae, "The Issue of Standing in Benefit-Cost Analysis", *Journal of Policy Analysis and Management*, Vol. 5, No. 4, 1986, pp. 665-682.

Wickizer, T., "Effects of Utilization Review on Hospital Use and Expenditures, A Review of the Literature and an Update on Recent Findings", *Medical Care Review*, Vol. 47, 1990, p. 327.

World Bank, *World Development Report 1993, Investing in Health* (N.Y.: Oxford University Press for the World Bank, 1993).